Beyond The Ice Cream Cone

Beyond The Ice Cream Cone

The Whole Scoop on Food at the 1904 World's Fair

Pamela J. Vaccaro, MA, CSP

Enid
PRESS
St. Louis

Beyond the Ice Cream Cone: The Whole Scoop on Food at the 1904 World's Fair

By Pamela J. Vaccaro, MA, CSP

Front Cover Design by Jean Lopez.
Back Cover Design by Trese Gloriod.
Front Cover Photo, courtesy Missouri Historical Society, St. Louis.
Back Cover Photo, Suzy Gorman Photography, St. Louis.
Book Interior by Jean Lopez, Lopez Needleman Graphic Design.
Book Production by Jean Lopez, Heather Needleman, and Trese Gloriod.
Composing Editor, Barbara Schmich Searle.
Copy Editor, Tom Evans.
Printing by Central Plains Book Manufacturing.

Published by Enid Press
          P.O. Box 16462
          St. Louis, Mo. 63125
          1-888-412-3953
          www.beyondtheicecreamcone.com

First edition April 2004
Printed in the United States of America

ISBN: 0-9745444-0-X

Dedicated to the American farmer,
whose contribution to the earth and its people
made the subject of this book possible.

TABLE OF CONTENTS

"A cheerful helpfulness
seems to be an American trait.
If you offered to carry a
countrywoman's lunch-basket
or her baby, she would consent
if she were really weary;
and, if you proved a pleasant
companion, she would invite
you to share her lunch."

Walter H. Page, *The World's Work 8*,
August, 1904.

In 1904, the largest World's Fair in history took place in St. Louis. Many nations of the world assembled on 1,272 beautifully landscaped acres to celebrate the purchase of the Louisiana Territory.

This enormous gathering brought together people from around the world, anxious to share their cultures. Pam Vaccaro's book deals with an important characteristic that assists in distinguishing one group of people from another: their food. She also shows how food can bring people together.

Food plays such a major role in our lives. Our language is filled with words like "potluck," "fast food," "buffet," "afternoon tea," "picnic," "Thanksgiving dinner," "finger food," "refreshments," "church supper," "birthday cake," and "snacks."

On the fairgrounds a century ago, I'm sure you could have overheard fairgoers ask the familiar question, "Where should we eat?"

The answer to that question would have had a variety of answers, including enjoying a picnic lunch from home, grabbing a quick lunch at one of the many food stands, or sitting down to an elaborate dinner in a beautiful restaurant. About 35,000 people could be served at the same time using all the food venues on the grounds.

A variation on the question could have been, "What do you want to eat?"

In this case, the answer would also have had multiple answers. In addition to the standard fare of American cuisine, participating countries brought exotic foods from their homeland and offered many choices. For the first time, fairgoers could experience different tastes, smells, and textures while eating foods with names they could not pronounce.

Pam Vaccaro presents a well-researched study of the food at the 1904 Louisiana Purchase Exposition. She tells us about everything from food venues to leftovers. She includes food facts and legends, famous food personalities, especially Sarah Tyson Rorer, turn-of-the-century recipes, and many human interest stories from one hundred years ago.

"Bon Appétit" as you devour this serving of interesting facts seasoned with tasteful stories about the food at the great 1904 World's Fair.

Max Storm, founder and president of the 1904 World's Fair Society,
co-author, *1904 Olympic Games Official Medals & Badges.*

PREFACE

THE object of this book is twofold: first, to present in a compact form a few of the choice recipes used at the Eastern Pavilion, at the Louisiana Purchase Exposition, St. Louis, 1904; and, secondly, to show how simply and easily all foods may be prepared. The object in teaching cookery is not to increase or complicate the work, not to make it a ceremonial, but to point out the simple and easy way.

SARAH TYSON RORER

World's Fair Souvenir Cook Book.
Author's collection.

1904

PREFACE

THE object of this book is twofold: first, to present a well-researched and compelling history of food at the Louisiana Purchase Exposition, St. Louis, 1904; and, secondly, to show how simply and easily food can bring the most diverse peoples to a common table. The object of this story is to broaden the perspective on how food came to be one of the many wonders of the 1904 World's Fair.

PAMELA J. VACCARO

2004

I'm not sure when I first became enamored with the 1904 World's Fair. Being a native St. Louisan, I grew up hearing stories about the Fair, especially during visits to Forest Park. As a student of history, I learned that its official name was, "The Louisiana Purchase Exposition," but it was always more than a name to me. I could imagine how exciting it must have been to pass through the turnstiles into a continual stream of interesting people and their creative endeavors.

I do know, however, exactly when my interest in food history began, how it developed, and how it eventually met my interest in the Fair. The two would have a rather long courtship, it turns out – over 20 years!

It was in 1971 that my dear friend Barbara Schmich and I sat in Plymouth Village in Mass. for an authentic Pilgrim breakfast of baked beans, cranberries, cornbread, fish cakes, and other out-of-the-ordinary fare. That was the beginning of my passion for food history, and my eighth and ninth grade history students back home would be the first to experience it. They used authentic cookbooks from that time period, prepared the recipes, and brought the fare to school for "Colonial Cooking Day."

Friends and family got a taste of my "historical cooking," too. Christmas Eve dinners were opportunities to create colonial dishes, cuisine of the post-bellum South, or even the 1946 Christmas day fare at a local military hospital. It wasn't until my brother's common-sense remark about the "little ones" in the family not taking a liking to 17th-century *hopping john* and 18th-century *gooseberry bomb* that the meals began to follow the traditional menu of turkey and mashed potatoes!

But it was a gift from my friend and fellow teacher, Joyce Coffey, that added a new dimension, the one that would directly affect the book you now hold in your hands. Always the master of finding the right holiday gift, she presented me with *Dining with William Shakespeare*, by Madge Lorwin, during the Christmas of 1978. Each chapter detailed the story of a contemporary food during the Elizabethan era and concluded with authentic recipes. This started a new flurry of historical meals at my home. There were the Renaissance dinners, feasts from the Middle Ages, and a Halloween fare using the recipes from an English witches' coven. Dinner guests were kind — appreciating my creative efforts and overlooking my less-than-mediocre ability to cook.

The summer of 1981 was when "it happened." The Vermont auctioneer yelled "sold," and passed the copy of the souvenir cookbook from the 1893 Chicago Columbian Exposition down the crowded row to where I was seated. If there was a Columbian souvenir cookbook, could there be a souvenir cookbook for the 1904 World's Fair? Trips to the Missouri Historical Society archives and the St. Louis Public Library produced the answer. Yes! A Mrs. Sarah Tyson Rorer had written the *World's Fair Souvenir Cook Book*. Was there more to the story of food at the Fair than the legends of the ice cream cone, the hot dog, and iced tea? Were those even true? I wondered.

In that same year, I made the decision to write a history of food at the Fair using the format of the Shakespeare book. Not long after, I took some initial steps. I visited the Missouri Historical Society library and archives and conducted oral histories with 80- and 90-year-olds who had been to the Fair. Their words were captured on tape and kept with my notes in a black leather notebook dedicated to this purpose. I also collected cookbooks of Mrs. Rorer, and gradually her life and impact on the world of food unfolded for me, as I believe it will for you with each chapter. I grew to appreciate what this woman brought to the Fair and was sure she would have a prominent place in my book.

But life got busy and the black leather notebook still sat on a shelf as a visible reminder; it was not until March 2003 that the project pushed its way back into my consciousness. I was actually planning to write a book about my work as a professional speaker in the area of time and attention management, which would certainly have been a more lucrative venture. But when my friend Linda Nash asked me over lunch one day, "How will you feel if you don't write the book on the Fair?," I knew there was no turning back. What life has taught me is that a truly creative dream cannot be left unattended. Writing the history of food at the Fair and including Mrs. Rorer's recipes would form the next chapter of my life.

The research was pure delight! Musty 100-year-old books and scrapbooks were my daily companions for months, and I lost all sense of time. Thousands of newspaper articles from 1901-1905 provided the small pieces of information I used as the basis for this book, and weeks of thought resulted in the overall plan for the book. Almost each day would produce a small fact from a "filler" article in a remote newspaper that made me hardly able to contain myself with excitement. I refrained from secondary sources because of the weak link they have proved to be in the story of food at the Fair. Except for what I believed were reputable Internet sources from reliable food historians, I stayed clear of secondary sources, always finding that most of them continued the culinary hearsay of the last 50-plus years.

And so, *Beyond the Ice Cream Cone: The Whole Scoop on Food at the 1904 World's Fair* came to be.

Beyond the Ice Cream Cone is a walk through the Fair on any given day and on some special days. Hopefully you will be amazed when you realize the enormity of the Fair and how it would dwarf any amusement in the world today. Hopefully these pages will make food at the Fair so real for you that you can almost taste the popular barbecued roast beef sandwiches or smell the freshly made caramel corn from the Popcorn Palace. Hopefully you will be able to imagine the sweet, intense flavor of popular drinks like grape juice or even a turn-of-the-century Budweiser. Hopefully you will sense what it would have been like to see the many exhibits and learn from the many food demonstrations. Hopefully you will get a glimpse of the fun that people had on the Pike.

Beyond the Ice Cream Cone does not take a linear approach to the Fair or the food at the Fair because the Fair itself begged the visitor to see as much as possible, but in any order that suited. Visitors would have likely seen the same things again and again on the way to something else. You, too, will be encountering some of the same people, places, and things several times as these pages unfold. Should you want a visual of your meanderings, pages 172–173 provide a detailed map. Fairgoers in 1904 used this map to orient themselves to exhibits, to events, or to locate the restaurants of their choice. Mrs. Rorer's restaurant was located to the left of Festival Hall, which is centrally located on the map.

Beyond the Ice Cream Cone represents my first book-writing journey, and "it

Hopefully you will be amazed when you realize the enormity of the Fair and how it would dwarf any amusement in the world today.

took a village" to assist me. My gratitude goes to the following people:

≈–Barbara Schmich Searle, composing editor, whose many talents as a counseling psychologist, artist, writer, and editor converged to shape and hone this manuscript, and who did so within the context of a 35-year friendship. Anna Searle, Barbara's daughter, who offered a fresh read on the material.

≈–Jean Lopez, a creative graphic designer and gifted artist who worked within my difficult time frame to design this book. I'm also thankful to Heather Needleman of Lopez Needleman Graphic Design for work on the production of this book. I have been fortunate to call them both "friend" for more than 20 years.

≈–Tom Evans, copy editor, whose unflappable nature was just what I needed while traversing this unknown terrain called "editing and re-editing."

≈–Trese Gloriod, graphic designer, who was called in to do some pinch-hitting and managed to hit home runs consistently on some final design and production issues.

≈–Sister Timothy Ryan, SSND, and Sister Francis Padberg, SSND, historians and teachers, who taught me the value of merging solid historical research with creative presentation.

≈–Bobbi Linkemer, experienced writer, author, editor, and supportive friend who guided me through the concept of writing a book and endured the first read of this manuscript.

≈–Pete Passanisi of Movere Publishing, friend and book development consultant. His excitement about my book has been insuppressible.

≈–Kathy Passanisi, professional speaker extraordinaire and my travel companion on this first-book journey — both of us kicking and screaming that we would rather speak than write a book. As always, her incredible humor dissolved my worst angst.

≈–Fawn Germer, author and "Peep" sister who saved a "Peep" in peril when she set aside her priorities to walk me through my first big "dark night of a writer's soul."

≈–Kim Kendall, friend and Internet researcher, who found a signed copy of the long-sought-after Mrs. Rorer's *World's Fair Souvenir Cook Book*. Her patience and prowess at using the Internet effectively also turned up information and memorabilia on Mrs. Rorer that I had never thought existed.

≈–Eileen Stretch, long-time friend and cooking enthusiast, who took time from her busy practice as a physician to select the appropriate recipes from the *World's Fair Souvenir Cook Book* to fit each chapter.

~—Max Storm, founder of the 1904 World's Fair Society and a collector who gave so many hours of his time and unreserved use of his outstanding collection of memorabilia. Without his generosity, the pages of this book would have been filled with many interesting facts begging for illustration. Shara (Jessie) Storm also contributed her photos and her enthusiasm.

~—Pat Villmer, Mike Truax, Louise Drescher, Lyndon Irwin, Yvonne Suess, and Fred Lavin, world's fair collectors who did not hesitate to offer their collections for use in my book. They helped this book come alive. Laura Brandt for her loan of World's Fair materials as well as all the many little things she did as a friend.

~—Jean Gosebrink, Special Collections specialist at the St. Louis Public Library, who dragged Exposition scrapbooks nearly her size back and forth while I put together my research. And Tom Pearson, who also assisted me.

~—Duane Sneddeker, director of library and archives at the Missouri Historical Society, for his assistance with research and illustrations, and his reminder when things went less than smoothly, that, "Anything worth doing is not always fun!"

~—Bob Miano, who was busy producing a documentary on the 1904 World's Fair, but never failed to help me out through my naiveté on photos and scans for this book.

~—Dr. Shannon Smith and his staff at the Missouri Botanical Garden in St. Louis, who took time from their world-renowned projects to analyze a photo of a "nut elephant" exhibit from the World's Fair.

~—My speakers' mastermind colleagues, Lois Creamer, Nancy Wegge, and Kathy Passanisi, who were truthful in their dislike about aspects of the book, but ready with applicable solutions.

~—My clients, who are wonderful advocates for my speaking profession, and who have already been supportive of this personal adventure. My speaker colleagues who have been cheering me on.

~—Vicki Pimentel, Nancy Lawing, Marti Sittner, and Chris Frederiksen, friends who called every few days while I was in my "seclusion" writing, just to see if I was doing well. Marcia Dajches, who has always been one of the most creative "answer persons" I know. Joan Corwin, who saved me hours of time working on the table of contents. Also, all my friends who are already starting to celebrate a book that has yet to arrive at my doorstep.

 ✒–Mary Conley and Frances Lynch, who were the first to hear the idea for this book, and who made it possible for me to call New England "home" for many summers.

 ✒–My three "furry" friends who remained constant companions and loved that I seemed to have nothing to do but stay home with them for two months.

 ✒–My family, who always wonders what I'm up to next, especially Peter and Theresa Vaccaro, my nephew and sister-in-law, who helped with production at the last minute.

 ✒–Most of all, a special thanks to my dad and mom, Guy and Jane Vaccaro, who, without exception, have been my biggest supports in life.

Sometimes people ask me, "What happened to fairs and food at the fairs after 1904?" Although food will never fall out of fashion, world's fairs have. There were other great fairs in the 20th century: San Francisco 1915, Chicago 1933, and New York 1939 and 1964. But things would change in the second half of the 20th century. Progress began happening at a much faster pace, and now invention happens so quickly that no fair could exhibit the latest of anything for seven months. By the time fairgoers would return home to unpack their bags, there would already be a second and third generation of most of the exhibited items.

But the 1904 World's Fair was a unique moment in human history because it really did present the progress of humankind to that point. As you will see in this book, it was not a "simpler" time. In many ways the Fair was extraordinarily complex and dwarfs most of the wonders of the contemporary world. But it was truly a prosperous and peaceful time, unsuspecting as its people were of the world conflict that would come in 1914.

 In that privileged time and place, one of the loftiest visions of any world's fairs was realized: welcoming diversity of all kinds, joining together for common ends, and creating — if only for seven months — an international community.

The Fair was not about eating. It was about a full menu of human experiences. But by looking at the Fair through the lens of food, I hope to have captured some of these experiences that endure, delight, and enrich our lives.

"It is not permissible to eat anything on the streets, even peanuts. A man devouring an orange or apple gets stared at and a young woman more so. ... But, at gala occasions the bar is raised. At circuses, summer gardens, and world's fairs, it is quite possible and proper to eat continuously from the time the gates open until they close."

St. Louis Globe-Democrat,
December, 1903.

Welcome to the Fair!

For seven months in 1904 it seemed as though everybody wanted to meet in St. Louis. More than 20 million people visited the magnificent World's Fair, spread over nearly 1,300 acres of land and encompassing more than 1,500 buildings. That's about 13 times the size of Walt Disney World's *Magic Kingdom*. Just thinking about walking that expanse of acreage works up a big appetite! But, for those who actually traversed the miles of fairgrounds and exhibit aisles, there were over 130 eateries to serve them when the need to feed their bodies outweighed the need to feed their minds!

A full century later people are still talking about the food at the Fair, but seldom does a discussion center around much more than trying to prove or disprove whether the World's Fair in St. Louis, and therefore the city itself, was the "birthplace" of certain foods — the ice cream cone, hot dog, hamburger, iced tea, or even sliced bread! It can be not only a lively topic of discussion but one that can bring a bit of defensiveness from the native population. With the benefit of having 100 years of hindsight — newspaper articles, scrapbooks, and published research about food at

The Fair's opening day, April 30, 1904, attracted 187,793 people.
Courtesy Max Storm.

the Fair — these questions will be addressed and answered in a new way in this book. Most important, they will be seen in the context of the whole Fair and all the food it offered.

The fare at the Fair provided something for everyone, no matter how sophisticated their taste or how limited their purse. The great abundance of food that was showcased at the Fair came from every corner of the earth and was wonderfully transformed by human inventiveness. The story of food at the Fair is as diverse and immensely interesting as the people who came to the Fair, and the Fair itself.

The Big Picture

Because people did not come to the Fair only to eat, it is important to know what they did with the rest of the time. The story of food would not be complete without knowing what visitors experienced at the Fair and how they managed to navigate among the many Fair attractions.

An average of 25,000 people boarded trains or trolleys every hour to get

The intramural railway wound through seven miles of the fairgrounds and had 17 stations to give fairgoers access to most of the attractions.
Courtesy Max Storm.

to the Fair in Forest Park. It cost 50 cents to go through the turnstile each day, approximately $10 in today's money. For $25 a person could get a season pass allowing him or her unlimited access to the Fair for seven months. Some people, e.g., stockholders and their guests, clergymen, and employees of local businesses, were given free passes to the Fair, while others jumped the turnstile or the fence. If caught, they typically claimed they had forgotten their money and had an engagement on the fairgrounds for which they did not want to be late.

However the fairgoer gained admission, the easiest way to get a general view of the fairgrounds was via the intramural railroad that wound through the grounds for seven miles. On that trip, the visitor would have gotten a taste of all the various kinds of attractions.

The Palaces

The Fair boasted 11 monumental "palaces" that showed historical and state-of-the-art human accomplishments. The palaces were: 1) Education and Social Economy, 2) Electricity, 3) Fine Arts, 4) Horticulture, 5) Agriculture, 6) Liberal Arts, 7) Transportation, 8) Manufactures, 9) Mines and Metallurgy, 10) Varied Industry, and 11) Machinery.

The palaces were enormous and the architecture unparalleled. But, except for the Palace of Fine Arts, all the massive palaces were fakes — made from staff, a mixture of plaster of Paris and a fibrous jute cloth. They were designed to captivate, but not to last.

State and Foreign Buildings

The fairgoer would also see at least some of the 42 individual state buildings and five territory buildings, which offered their visitors a "home away from home." An Oklahoma family took that to heart when they arrived at the Oklahoma building and asked the attendant where they should put their

bags! It was their territory's building, wasn't it? Although the state and territory buildings provided everything from free food to mail service, lodging wasn't a perk. The 62 buildings of the foreign nations and their colonies were so unique and colorful in their designs that the Exposition did not group them all together like most of the state buildings, but spaced them out to create more balance to the panoramic view of the Fair.

Exhibits

From the train one could obtain glimpses of some of the 70,000 exhibits. Indoor exhibits displayed everything from mechanical engines to the production of syrup. The train ride offered visitors a good look at the outdoor exhibits, including 37 livestock areas, an English bowling green, and a floral clock that operated on the principles of a sun dial — with flowers opening up at different times of day.

There was even a "Model Street," with buildings such as the Model Hospital, Model Library, Model Nursery, Model Playground, Model Restaurant, and so on. The Exposition was quite taken with the idea of prototypes, and each showed the finest advances in its industry.

The Floral Clock on the north side of Palace of Agriculture was a popular meeting place.
Courtesy Max Storm.

The St. Louis World's Fair tried something that broke rank from previous world's fairs — "live people exhibits," which showed native peoples from Africa, Asia, and America going about their daily activities of working, playing, and, of course, eating. Visitors could also see both Indian and Philippine natives sitting in wooden school desks, learning from an American teacher. In 1904, the live people exhibits were another display of U.S. achievement — people whose lives were better because of American "assistance."

U.S. Government Attractions

The U.S. government sponsored several attractions. The Government Building displayed miniature warships showing the day-to-day movement of all the country's vessels. There were also displays of government-sponsored food experiments identifying contaminants or "adulterations," as they called them. In addition, a huge outdoor bird cage, which contained every species of bird in the nation, allowed fairgoers to enter and see the birds closeup.

The roller chair was one of the favorite ways to get around at the Fair.
Courtesy Max Storm.

Getting Ready for the Fair

It quickly became apparent that the Fair was only for the fit — those who were physically, mentally, and financially able to meet the challenge of exploring "the world" in a day or a week. Although some people could afford to rent an electric automobile or a "roller chair" (a kind of baby carriage for adults), most walked many miles to visit the buildings and attractions that drew their interest.

Physical Preparation

When one visitor, Katherine Glover, returned home to Georgia after her visit to the Fair, she warned her friends to get themselves in shape and to bring the kinds of shoes their grandmothers would wear at home when they knew no one was coming for tea. In her article "Hints to Prospective Visitors to the Great St. Louis Exposition," she wrote, "I suggest these things with a prompting of human sympathy that comes of tired, blistered feet, and a brain reeling from the sight of so many things at once. I have just been to the Fair."

She wasn't kidding. Just seeing the rows of exhibits in the 22-acre Palace of Agriculture required nine miles of walking! "You should begin by trying to see how long you can stand on your feet each day," Mrs. Glover advised. "If your feet

Strolling along Jefferson Way took these walkers past the Palace of Education.
Courtesy Max Storm.

5

become so numb with pain that you don't care whether you sit or stand, live or die, I should advise that you begin a practice of walking a few dozen miles a day until you get in 'exposition trim' of 50 miles a day."

Phoenix Hotel,
1412 OLIVE ST.

Home Cooking, Meals Like Mother Used to Cook.
Meals Served All Hours from 6 a. m. to 11 p. m.
MEALS, – 25c.
Board and Room–$1 50 per Day, and up, Including Lunch to take to the Fair.

The Phoenix Hotel was one of the establishments approved by the Exposition and recommended to out-of-town visitors.

Fiscal Preparation

The physical challenge was just one hurdle. Money was another. Mrs. Glover advised: "Be sure to scrape up all the money you can possibly lay your hands on, and a little more, then still a little more; and having learned the art of shaving a dollar and a half Exposition appetite down to a fifty-cent lunch, I should say you are in excellent trim for thorough enjoyment of the great Fair." The cost of lodging, entrance fees, and food alone averaged $4 to $5 each day, which in today's money is upwards of $100 per day.

Mental Preparation

The sheer size of the Fair was yet another hurdle. Jim Foley, a North Dakota newspaperman, warned his readers that not planning ahead was a mistake. "If you go down to the Fair without a definite idea of what you want to see you won't see as much as you would if you adopt the plan of the systematic sight seer." One man who apparently did not plan well was noted by T. Sapp, Jr., in a St. Paul newspaper. Mr. Sapp had seen a visitor at one of the entry gates demanding a refund of $5.40 for the $6 he had paid. When the gatekeeper asked what justified a refund, the man said, "I've been here for two weeks and seen only about one-tenth of the Fair, and I paid to see it all. The thing is so all-fired big that I've missed nine-tenths of the sights, and if you don't gimme back $5.40, I'll sue the company."

Katherine Glover described the kind of focus required of a successful fairgoer: "It seems to me a good thing to do would be to try the trick of looking at one thing with one eye and another with the remaining fellow [the other eye], at the same

time taking notes on a third thing with the right hand and fingering a fourth object with the left." Another 1904 advisor suggested more simply that, "a good division of the day is to give the freshest hours of it to whatever building interests the visitor most, and, after luncheon, make a less severe tax on the attention."

Enjoying the End of the Day

"About 5 you will certainly have learned the gentle Exposition art of 'flopping' — falling limp on any conceivable object that offers the slightest opportunity for sitting. About 8 you should join the great army of 'floppers' that are thick all over the grounds." So said Mrs. Glover. There were, however, many attractions that could be saved for the end of the day, even though they were good places to visit at any time.

Festival Hall

Festival Hall was a great place for visitors to sit, close their eyes, and listen to the music of famous composers from around the world. The world's largest pipe organ was built inside Festival Hall and bellowed out the classical music of the ages. It was hard to beat the band when it came to the most popular music of the Exposition.

From Berlin to Boston and all points around, famous bands came to entertain both music aficionados and those who just liked to tap their feet.

The Lagoons

Equally relaxing was renting a gondola or a "motorboat" and taking a ride in the lagoons around the "Main Picture" — the view of the Fair that included Festival Hall, a colonnade, the Terrace of States, and two restaurant rotundas.

Fairgoers took to sightseeing via water in gondolas or motorboats. The lagoons and Grand Basin provided one and one-half miles of waterway views of the Fair.

Courtesy Max Storm.

Visitors could have gone anytime during the day, but the ride in the evening was lit by millions of electric lights draping the palaces, a first for any World's Fair!

The Pike

A most popular end-of-the-day attraction was "The Pike," a mile-long string of cafes, concessions, restaurants, and amusements that had an international theme. A fairgoer could walk the "Streets of Cairo" and go "via ship" from "New York to the South Pole." He could ride a camel down the street, go skating in a snow storm, see Hagenbeck's Trained Animals, and then visit the miniature Alps and eat at a Tyrolean restaurant. The Pike seems harmless today, but it provided its share of controversies in 1904 because there were

The mile-long strip of amusements and restaurants along the Pike offered something for everyone who attended the Fair.
Courtesy Max Storm.

The Pike had an international theme, and fairgoers could ride camels or elephants on the streets of the "Mysterious Asia" attraction.
Courtesy Max Storm.

fortunetellers at one end of the Pike and medical experimentation at the other. The Incubator Exhibit displayed premature infants being cared for by nurses trained in using this medical innovation. When the infant was well enough, it was taken from the display. While Alice Roosevelt, daughter of the president, found it compelling to "do" the Pike, a writer for *World's Work* found it repelling. "One visit is enough to see the Pike for most normal persons; for most of these 'shows' are very stale and commonplace."

No doubt you've heard the expression, "Coming down the pike," which had its origin at the 1904 World's Fair. Nobody knew what was coming next. The variety of attractions and foods could be overwhelming, exhilarating, or offensive, depending on your point of view.

The Ralston Purina Co. of St. Louis gave these complimentary pasteboard boxes to anyone visiting its booth in the Palace of Agriculture.

Courtesy Max Storm (Permission from company).

You Will Never Forget the WORLD'S FAIR and your Ralston Box

St. Louis World's Fair 1904

The postcard from Mrs. Rorer's restaurant read: "In this pavilion Mrs. Rorer, the famous cook who often writes receipts [recipes] for the Ladies Home Journal serves dinners and luncheons. Harriet tried 'em tho. E.E.R."

Courtesy Max Storm.

Sharing the Fair

1904 travelers, like most adventurers, wanted to take a visual piece of the experience home with them. Some might need a trinket to placate the disappointment or ire of those left behind; others might have sensed the historic nature of the event and wanted a commemoration. One of Mrs. Glover's concrete suggestions was to acquire a Ralston Purina box in the Agriculture building. This "Purina bag " as Mrs. Glover called it would hold the many free things — including lots of food samples — given to them by exhibitors, in addition to the souvenirs they purchased.

Postcards were popular items to send to people back home, and the bags of postal workers were stuffed every day but Sunday, when the Fair was closed. Another item in great demand was Sarah Tyson Rorer's *World's Fair Souvenir Cook Book*. Her name was a household word in America at that time because of her popular column in the *Ladies' Home Journal*. Eating at her restaurant was something to write home about, and having her sign her cookbook made it a special souvenir for almost any woman and many men.

If the mention of cookbooks and restaurants and lots of physical and mental activity is working up your appetite, you are in the right mindset for reading on and finding out more about food at the Fair.

Mrs. Rorer signed all her communications and her World's Fair Souvenir Cook Book with, "Yours very truly, Sarah Tyson Rorer."

Author's collection.

CHAPTER 2

Everyone Ate at the Fair

Men, women, and children came to the 1904 World's Fair from all parts of the globe. They came from Siam and St. Louis, from the Philippines and Paris. Some wore turbans; others donned top hats. Some women wore satin and lace and others wore practical cotton shirtwaists. At first glance, there seemed to be no common denominator among them. Yet there was one profoundly simply human activity they shared — everyone ate at the Fair.

Food was important to the Exposition from its first to its last days. In fact, during the three-year planning and building stage before the Fair opened, hundreds of thousands of people "ate at the Fair." Millions ate at the Fair during the seven months it was open to the public. Finally, thousands more ate at the Fair while it was being dismantled and was vanishing into memory and myth.

The Planners

The very beginning of the Fair took place in the context of eating. On June 7, 1896, David R. Francis, a St. Louis businessman, former mayor of St. Louis, and former governor of Missouri, walked to his monthly meeting of the St. Louis Business Men's League. He planned to propose an idea over lunch when his colleagues were relaxed — a World's Fair in St. Louis. "There is one event in the history of this city second in importance only to the Declaration of Independence … and that is the Louisiana Purchase." With these words, Francis, who would become the Fair's president, initiated one of the most significant events in international cooperation during peacetime: the Louisiana Purchase Exposition, also known as the 1904 St. Louis World's Fair.

St. Louis was one of the few Expositions to select a theme for its Fair that was

> Food was important to the Exposition from its first to its last days. In fact, during the three-year planning and building stage before the Fair opened, hundreds of thousands of people "ate at the Fair." Millions ate at the Fair during the seven months it was open to the public. Finally, thousands more ate at the Fair while it was being dismantled and was vanishing into memory and myth.

directly related to the city. The Louisiana Purchase had doubled the size of the United States and included the land that would become Missouri. Lewis and Clark, explorers of this new territory, started their journey in St. Louis. It was there that they ate their last meals in familiar surroundings and there that they were outfitted with the food staples needed for the expedition. It was also in nearby St. Charles, Mo., that the explorers purchased the whiskey that made them drunk the night before their trip. The 1904 World's Fair was to stand in a tradition of exploration, expansion, and conviviality.

Inviting People to the Party

It literally took an act of Congress to get permission to have the St. Louis World's Fair. In 1901, Congress granted approval for the Louisiana Purchase Exposition (LPE) of 1903, the actual anniversary of the Louisiana Purchase. Because of the scope of the preparations, however, it had to be postponed until 1904. During the planning process, there was a continuous stream of business luncheons, receptions, teas, banquets, and dinners.

Fair President Francis and some of the World's Fair commissioners to Europe met in London for a conference. Florence Hayward was the only woman with any official leadership role during the Fair. President David R. Francis is seated in the center of the first row.
Courtesy Max Storm.

So many people needed to be wined and dined: potential stockholders who would need to underwrite the Fair, congressmen who would need to vote for federal aid, and philanthropists who would need to be impressed with the probable impact of the Fair. In addition, potentates and premiers of foreign countries needed to be convinced that participation with the LPE was worth their time and money. This last job was the responsibility of state and foreign commissioners. All were men except one, Florence Hayward of the Board of Lady Managers, who was commissioner primarily to Britain but also to France, Germany, and Holland. She was a graduate of Mary Institute, a branch of Washington University at the time, and a frequent contributor to *Vanity Fair* and *Harper's*, as well as to the *St. Louis Post-*

Louisiana Purchase Exposition Co.

Dedicatory Excursion

To *Pan - American Exposition*

.. July 2, 1901 ..

Leave St. Louis . 2.30 p m, June 30th   Leave Buffalo . . 2.30 p m, July 4th
Arrive Buffalo . . 8.00 a m, July 1st   Arrive St. Louis . 8.00 a m, July 5th

- - - VIA - - -

C. C. C. & St. L. and Lake Shore Roads.

Pullman Dining Car Service

DINNER

Mock Turtle	Consomme, Clear
Cucumbers	Young Onions

Baked Lake Trout, Fine Herbs

Potatoes Parisienne

Soft Shell Crabs on Toast   Baked Spaghetti, Italienne

Prime Roast Beef, Au Jus

Roast Duckling

Boiled Potatoes	Braised Sweet Potatoes
Green Corn	Buttered Beets

Lobster Salad, au Mayonnaise

Chilled Water Melon

Neapolitan Ice Cream	Assorted Cake
Marmalade	English Wafers
Canadian and Edam Cheese	Bent's Water Crackers

Coffee   Tea   Iced Tea

En Route, June 30, 1901.

The planners enjoyed three meals a day in the Pullman Dining Car as they made their way to the Pan-American Exposition in 1901.

Courtesy Missouri Historical Society, St. Louis.

Dispatch and the *St. Louis Republic*.

The commissioners got permission from the Exposition's executive committee to take certain actions while traveling abroad, including approval for "meal expenses." Since time was of the essence and security was an issue, each commissioner received a copy of the *Private Cipher Code*. This manual listed codes they could use to communicate messages to the committee. When August Busch, the commissioner to Germany, wanted to offer the Germans more than a "Bud" while discussing their participation in the Fair, he would wire, "OAKFIEL 51332." Decoded, this meant, "I think it wise to give a dinner here to some of the government and municipal authorities and prominent newspaper reporters and some others, in all about (inserted number of people). It will cost approximately (inserted cost)." The committee would return a coded message to Busch either giving or denying him permission, limiting the expenditures, or requesting more information before the committee could make its decision. The commissioners knew well the political influence of the dining table.

The Top Brass on a Field Trip

The city of Buffalo, N.Y., was hosting an international exposition the very year St. Louis received the go-ahead for the LPE. The Buffalo Pan-American Exposition in 1901 would afford them the opportunity to learn from that city's successes and mistakes, and to do a little marketing for the LPE.

In the summer of 1901, the Exposition leaders took a trip to Buffalo, and they traveled in style. They dined in the state-of-the-art Pullman Dining Car. At each meal, the Fair organizers enjoyed fine food in multiple courses, a practice that was familiar to them as successful business leaders.

Camaraderie

The committees in St. Louis met frequently over lunch, welcomed their comrades home from foreign travel, and even celebrated landmarks in each other's lives. When August Busch returned from Germany, the committee he chaired had a reception and banquet in his honor to celebrate his success at getting Germany to "sign on the dotted line."

Frederick V. Skiff's relationships with his LPE associates were good examples of the kind of camaraderie that was possible among the men and women. The Field Museum in Chicago "loaned" him to St. Louis for seven months in 1904, and he directed the important job of defining the role of exhibits at the Fair. His comrades were well aware of the heavy burden he carried as he left for Europe to meet potential exhibitors — the recent loss of his only child. Although they could not relieve him of his sadness when leaving, they managed to assure him that he was welcomed home. A luncheon was held in his honor. Skiff was on the giving end as well, throwing a bachelor party and then a farewell dinner for his popular young assistant. On the very day after the Fair closed in December, Skiff left for his home in Chicago, but not without a farewell banquet for him hosted by Francis.

Travel and time away from home became a lifestyle for these planners. Especially at these times, they represented home for each other. Their work was hard, and a morning breakfast or an evening meal together provided more than an opportunity to further the goals of the LPE. It developed lasting friendships. For many years the Exposition leaders met at an annual banquet to celebrate the memories of 1904, as Francis had envisioned: "The reunion will be repeated, I trust, from year to year as long as two or more of our members may live to get together."

The Workers

The workforce was filled with laborers and craftsmen with varying degrees of experience. They were men and women of many nationalities. Some were independent workers and others were members of a still-new idea in America — the labor union. They each brought a different talent, and they all ate at the Fair.

Fare for the Fair Builders

About 200,000 people showed up each day to build more than 1,500 buildings that were designed to last for less than a year and yet look like they had been built to last for centuries. Most construction workers, whose time and budgets were limited, carried graniteware lunch pails and ate at their work areas.

The Exposition leadership intended to give permission for certain restaurants to open before the Fair did. Because they were slow to do this, workers had few options other than to bring their own lunches. The first to complain loudly were the female employees in the Administration Building. They complained that they had to walk all the way to Clayton, University City, or take the trolly downtown to St. Louis to get a nice meal during work hours. This was highly impractical because they were allowed only one hour for lunch. To solve the problem, the Exposition granted a concession to Charles Marchiatti to build a restaurant a short distance from the Administration Building. They called it, appropriately, the Administration Restaurant. It was one of the larger restaurants with sections for those who wanted fine dining and those who wanted a good meal at a reasonable price.

The Power of the Press

Fifty-three thousand foreign and U.S. news correspondents covered the thousands of publicity events occurring during the Fair. Newspeople played a vital role.

What they wrote created indelible images in the minds of readers, both the ones who came to the Fair in person as well as the others who experienced it only through the reporters' eyes. Because food was such a major attraction, much was written about it. These reports help give us an authentic view of the role food played at the Fair.

The mighty force of the press swarmed the fairgrounds and the Pike every minute of every day, looking for prominent lead stories to put in prominent newspapers like the *Chicago Tribune* and the *New York Times*, or for obscure incidents to serve as fillers in equally obscure food trade journals like the *Retail Butchers Journal,* the *Orange Juice Farmer*, or the *New England Grocer*. These journalists functioned like magnets, with every country, state, and company — both foreign and domestic — vying for media attention. Politicians, business leaders, investors, and socialites also angled to get their names and faces in print.

Members of the press were guests of the German commissioner at the German Gast Haus.
Courtesy Max Storm.

For example, Theodore Lewald, Germany's imperial representative to the Fair, was commissioned to show his country in the very best light possible. The German government wanted to outshine its European neighbors. To ensure as much exposure as possible during the Fair, Lewald hosted a dinner for the Fair's corps of newspapermen at the Gast Haus near the German Pavilion. He made sure that the most influential editors were in attendance, including representatives from all four major St. Louis papers at that time: The *Post-Dispatch*, the *Republic*, the *Globe-Democrat,* and the *St. Louis Mirror*. Also in attendance were Mark Bennitt of the General Press Bureau and Frank Stockbridge of the *New York American*, who would collaborate on the highly regarded *History of the Louisiana Purchase Exposition* in 1905. Lewald was very smart to include Colin Selph from the *World's Fair Bulletin*, published by the Missouri Historical Society. Editors of the *Bulletin* praised Lewald's efforts by saying, "The menu was the highest acme of culinary art, and the wines of old and magnificent vintage." The banquet ended with newsmen congratulating Germany and its leadership for its prominent participation in the Exposition.

The Protectors

It is almost impossible to calculate the value of the treasures on display within the 1,272-acre fairgrounds. There had been 12,000 train cars filled with exhibits that had been delivered to the Fair.

King Edward VII of England allowed his mother's (Queen Victoria's) jubilee presents to be on display, and Philadelphia carefully packaged the Liberty Bell to be sent to St. Louis. But "treasure" is, of course, in the eyes of the beholder. The fruitgrower from California who brought his 2.5-pound, 18-inch-round orange, the largest ever grown, considered it priceless, too — fit for display to both countryman and foreigner, and worthy of being protected.

The Jefferson Guard

The "top guns," so to speak, were 600 members of the Jefferson Guard under the direction of the U.S. Army. The Guard's primary job was to protect the investments of those from all over the world who were participating in the Fair and to keep order on the fairgrounds. They arrived during construction and stayed through demolition.

Fortunately, the Guard members had to spend more time chasing people who jumped the turnstiles than they did hunting actual art thieves. The most frequently confiscated "weapon" was an illegally sized camera or tripod. Because the Exposition granted concession rights to a few official Fair photographers, no one could bring a camera on the fairgrounds that produced negatives larger than 4 inches by 5 inches. The Guard would warn the fairgoer or confiscate the camera if necessary. They were also responsible for catching smokers lighting up any place but inside the cafes and restaurants where the habit was permitted.

Feeding the Guard

The Jefferson Guard would enjoy their fare at the Fair. The Exposition saw to that when it signed a contract with the Army to supply a mess hall and provide meals for 35 cents. However, the Exposition wanted control over the menu, and this ended up improving the quantity and quality of Guard's food.

The Jefferson Guard, as well as this calvary unit, regarded their assignments as a "rare treat and entered upon their duties with enthusiasm."

Author's collection.

The Feb. 23, 1904, edition of the *Post-Dispatch* listed the contract details and the bill of fare. The dishes chosen were intended to make the soldiers think they were eating in a country farmhouse. Meals were not to be served in courses, but rather placed on the tables "country style" so the soldiers could see at the outset what they would be eating. According to the contract, cakes, pies, and puddings were to be served each day at dinner; the practice of having such desserts on hand was a novelty at that time. Colonel E.C. Culp, who had served in the Civil War, sent letters to officers outlining these unusual conditions and adding that he had never enjoyed such good food during his entire time in the field. Of course, the Fair was hardly a combat zone!

The Visitors

Travel agents and travel companies knew very well how to entice the fairgoer to St. Louis. Ads for railroad and boat excursions detailing the comforts of their services appeared in thousands of publications. Food was not considered a perk, but a necessity. The quality of food, physical surroundings, and special service added to the value.

Courtesy of Max Storm.

The Mobile and Ohio Railroad had a reputation for being progressive, efficient, and luxurious. The company was highly competitive in getting the St. Louis travel market to and from the South. Its 1902 dining car had great appeal for travelers. The walls were made of highly polished quartered oak, and the fixtures were made of shiny brass. Five people could sit at a table. The cars were lit by electricity and cooled by electric fans, which made them very modern indeed.

But it was the service that made a trip on the railroad so compelling. Each car had a conductor, a chef, an assistant, and three waiters. The service included cut glass, china, and linens. In order to please the most finicky eater, all the meals were a la carte. The *Mirror* had high praises for the Mobile and Ohio dining car and even its menu card: "The menu-card … contains everything that the most fastidious gourmet is accustomed to. Prices however are reasonable and moderate. The menu caters to the rich as well as the people of limited means. A feature of the dining service is that the Citronelle Springs water is used exclusively. The wine list is ideal, and that means a good deal."

The Rich and the Famous

Most Fair visitors were "regular folks" — they may have saved for a whole year to attend for just one day. However, others in attendance made enough money in one day to attend the Fair for almost a year. For the elite, their very presence brought so much attention that the Exposition officials and other dignitaries prepared receptions or banquets in their honor and even dedicated whole days to them.

Geronimo was both an exhibit and an exhibitor at the Fair.
Courtesy Max Storm.

Others were not rich, but they had "household names." Such well-recognized people as Dorothea Dix, the famous social reformer for the mentally challenged, Helen Keller and her teacher, Anne Sullivan, and future President William Howard Taft visited the Fair. Geronimo and Chief Joseph were featured guests in the Indian exhibits. Geronimo was there through most of the Fair, probably taking his meals from the Indian School dining room, where food was prepared for demonstration and eaten by the residents of the Indian Territory Building. Geronimo met his daughter Lena there. He had not seen her since she was an infant; one can only imagine that a shared meal followed this sweet reunion.

Some visitors were both rich and famous, such as the members of the charismatic Roosevelt family. Teddy Roosevelt, who was president at the time, came to the dedication in 1903 and returned for President's Day in late November 1904. In between, his children visited the Fair and brought nearly as much attention as the president himself.

Alice Roosevelt and Mayor Wells of St. Louis drive to one of the 12 events held in honor of Alice's three-day visit to the Fair.

Courtesy Max Storm.

Alice Roosevelt

When Roosevelt's daughter Alice arrived at the Fair on the afternoon of May 26, she was immediately escorted to a reception at the house of Daniel Catlin of Vandeventer Place. During her stay, she sometimes traveled incognito, and, at other times, in full style as a dignitary. Alice had adopted her father's philosophy — *carpe diem*. The *Republic* reported her "shocking" behavior as she exited the train: she lit up a cigarette! She was not prone to convention in any way, and her father was quick to say of her: "I can run the country, or I can control Alice. I just can't do both." So it should have been no surprise that the 20-year-old dashed off to the Pike with her friend Irene Catlin and a band of young people during the two hours after her welcoming reception. They remained at the Pike until the gates closed at 11:30 p.m.

An international ball was given in Alice's honor at the palatial German Pavilion. She dined with the Board of Lady Managers and attended the reception at the dedication of the Illinois Building. Wherever she went, she received honors and gifts. The chiefs of Filipino tribes entertained her with dancing.

Within three days, Alice attended nearly a

Alice Roosevelt was the official guest of Fair President Francis and Mrs. Francis.

Courtesy Max Storm.

dozen receptions, luncheons, and formal dinners. She received almost more honors than her father or the heir prince of China. On her final trip to the Pike, she rode a donkey down the street, climbed the Tyrolean Alps, had her fortune told by a dark-skinned wizard in the streets of Cairo, and learned from him that she was soon to be married to a blond multimillionaire. Two years later, Alice married dark-haired Nicholas Longworth, who was better known for gathering maidens than millions. So goes the authenticity of some of the amusements on the Pike!

Alice was the guest of honor at a very exclusive dinner given by the commissioner from France, Michel Lagrave, at his residence in the 2800 block of Lindell. A number of St. Louis debutantes attended, including Irene Caitlin. The meal was served in a beautifully decorated apartment, opening into a magnificent drawing room. Miss Roosevelt occasioned no little surprise from her host by her easy command of the French language. The menu included gourmet French cuisine — Consommé a la Chartres and Tartietles a la Paisa. The vintage wines and sherries dated from 1870 to 1890. To honor the presence of the president's daughter, the candied fruit glaze and the cake were given her last name — Glacé Roosevelt and Gateaux Roosevelt.

The Roosevelt Boys

Alice's younger brothers and cousin visited the Fair in July 1904. Much like their older sister, Teddy Jr. (17) and Kermit (15) were both impetuous and respectful. These were the same boys who used large pans from the White House kitchen to "sled down" the inside steps and the same boys who were caught using portraits of former presidents for peashooter targets. Nothing should have surprised the Fair managers.

The Café Luzon was located inside the Philippine Exhibit and was the favorite restaurant of President Roosevelt's sons.
Courtesy Louise Drescher.

On one of the days of their visit, Harry Watcham, manager of the Inside Inn, planned a reception for the Roosevelt boys to be held on the second floor balcony of the inn at 9:30 a.m. Twenty prominent people attended the breakfast minus the boys, however, who were far more eager to see the Fair. At 9 a.m., they had sneaked out and made a beeline to the Philippine Village to see the big attraction, the Igorots, who were natives of the Philippines. Some smart Fair organizer realized the boys' interest and planned a luncheon at the Café Luzon inside the Philippine Village. Although the boys often followed their inclinations instead of protocol, they did manage to graciously thank their hosts, and they were on time when they dined with Fair President Francis at the Director's Club in the West Restaurant Pavilion.

A Prince of a Guy at the Fair

When Prince Pu Lun, heir apparent to the throne of China, visited the Fair, he was a young man who must have been taught to say, "beautiful ladee," whenever he found himself in a situation with American socialites. In an interview with the *Omaha Nebraska Daily News*, his interpreter remarked that his highness was delighted with this country but was overwhelmed by the amount of food.

Prince Pu Lun of China was one of the first prominent foreign visitors to the Fair.
Courtesy Max Storm.

The prince's interpreter explained, "He [Prince Pu Lun] marvels greatly at the pace the Americans set for him. He says he would much like to eat and drink all the food and all the liquids that you have set before him, but he is not a large man and he is not used to so much food and entertainment. Since he has landed in this country he has been whirled from one reception to another, from breakfast to luncheon, from luncheon to dinner, and from dinner to banquet, with receptions between times, at which more lunch and more punch is served. He likes American food, and he thinks American drinks are the nectar of the gods, but he realizes sadly that he is human and that the capacity of the human stomach is limited."

Infants and Children

Children of fairgoers could be guaranteed a healthy, hearty meal if they were cared for at the Fair's Model Nursery or the Model Playground.

At the Model Nursery, trained nurses cared for the infants in the "Baby Cottage." While moms or dads were out sightseeing, the nurses fed the babies sterilized milk and scientific infant foods, equivalent to our natural foods today. When the mothers returned, they could watch trained technicians in the nursery's laboratory kitchen teaching them ways to prepare scientific baby food. If a mother wished to take her baby with her, she could rent an "infant perambulator" —- a baby buggy — for 25 cents.

Some parents left their older children at the Model Playground. The adults received a "kid check" and needed to return it for proof of "ownership" when they picked the child up at the end of sightseeing. The children enjoyed play and were fed two meals a day on pure "scientific" foods advocated by Mrs. Hirshfield, director of the playground.

Each day, 20 to 50 children strayed from their parents. One of the duties of the Jefferson Guard was to bring lost children to the Model Playground, where they were immediately fed milk and bread. By late September, nearly 500 lost children had made their way to the playground. Repeat visitors may have actually caught on to the benefits of "getting lost"!

The "call to dinner" is a welcome sound in any culture. This Negrito from the Philippines used a tom-tom similar to those used in lunchrooms at train stations in 1904.

Author's collection.

The Igorots

The Igorots were one of a number of what the Fair organizers referred to as the "uncivilized peoples." The U.S. had acquired the Philippines and Puerto Rico just a few years before the Fair opened, and, after getting the spoils from the Spanish-American War, the country was given more to imperialism. The U.S. was proud of its achievement and thought about how it could benefit from the foreign peoples who inhabited the new additions to the country's map. By inviting the Igorots, the Moros, and the Negritos to the Fair and observing their daily rituals, the planners and visitors were acting authentically for their time and place in history.

A local newspaper reported on the diet of the Igorots: "The Village people are well fed. Each member has three bananas a day and all the rice, sweet potatoes, coffee and meat he wishes. Beef, chicken, and pork are their favorite meats. Dog meat is served to villagers who are ill. Watermelons, apples, turnips, rutabagas and cabbage give variety in fruit and vegetables. They cultivate rice, sweet potatoes, tobacco, corn, coffee and sugar cane and raise chickens and pigs in their native land. Bananas and cocoa nuts grow wild. Both males and females receive all the tobacco they wish."

Some St. Louisans were aghast that the Igorots' diet included dog meat at the time of illness and on certain other occasions according to their customs. Like a tragic highway accident that compels someone to slow down his car and look, most fairgoers could not resist watching these foreign peoples break from familiar culinary mores. This occasional bill of fare for the Igorots fashioned a stream of controversy among St. Louisans and a continued fascination for many more years. Our inviting them to the Fair at all is now equally controversial.

Courtesy Max Storm.

Food, The Great Equalizer

It would be hard to imagine the variety of chance encounters people had at the Fair, but no doubt food played an important part in them. A farmer from Missouri might lunch at the Model Dairy counter with a banker from Boston. Women from different parts of the country or the world might have exchanged recipes. A particularly pointed story tells of John Brisben Walker, an editor for *Cosmopolitan*, who was tired from walking all day at the Fair. He rented a roller chair for 50 cents and engaged in conversation with the young roller chair boy, a Methodist seminarian, who pushed the chair. It was the policy of the company to hire educated young men to carry on proper discourse with their clients. Walker and the young man crossed the small boundary that existed between them and went to the Chinese restaurant on the Pike, where they talked the evening away. Such was the nature of the Fair. In those moments, the world got smaller and people's visions became broader.

CHAPTER 3

Concessionaires and Their Wares

If the palaces and exhibits enlightened and amazed the minds of the fairgoers, the concessions offered solutions to their more basic needs. Officially the term "concession" meant "any line of business conducted upon the Exposition grounds for the purposes of gain, whether the object of such business is the comfort of the public or its amusement or entertainment." If there was a cash register connected to a display or booth, the Exposition's Division of Concessions and Admissions played a role in putting it there.

The Process

Norris B. Gregg, director of the Division of Concessions and Admissions, oversaw the committee that had the power to accept or reject applications for concessions. To secure a concession at the Exposition, applicants had to conform to the process set by the Committee on Concessions, which met weekly at the Mercantile Building or the Laclede Building in downtown St. Louis. There they considered applications for every concession on the grounds, including those that involved food. Many meetings were relatively routine, but others included passionate presentations by applicants determined to secure a lucrative spot at the Fair. If the committee blessed the application, it went to the Executive Committee of the Exposition for final approval.

> The committee's purpose was twofold: to select concessions that would best serve fairgoers and to find concessions with the greatest promise of financial profit.

The committee's purpose was twofold: to select concessions that would best serve fairgoers and to find concessions with the greatest promise of financial profit. The Louisiana Purchase Exposition Company (LPE Co.) was a publicly owned corporation that had been given a limited charter by the state of Missouri. Ultimately, the committee granted concessions to 600 individuals or companies, which added about $3 million to the LPE Co.'s coffers. This amount nearly paid off the $4.5 million loan the LPE Co. received from Congress, which had been a major source of startup funds for the Fair.

Agreements

The Exposition expected concessionaires to pay a rental fee commensurate with the number and size of the booths, their location on the fairgrounds, and the size of their operations, which ranged from four feet by four feet to entire buildings. They also paid the company a minimum of 25 percent of their gross receipts.

The Exposition supplied lighting, electricity, water, refrigeration, and compressed air, but concessionaires were charged for these services at rates established by the Exposition's Division of Works. This division, directed by the highly regarded Isaac Taylor, also regulated the way concessionaires could build their booths and buildings as well as how they disposed of their garbage.

Every concessionaire received a copy of the *General Rules Governing Concessionaires*. The rules were straightforward and strict: "No business under any of the concessions shall be conducted in any other than a first class orderly manner. No gambling or games of chance will be allowed anywhere within the Exposition Grounds. All goods sold must be what they are represented to be and no deception will be allowed. All supply wagons must perform deliveries between the hours of 5 a.m. and 8 a.m. Only articles as are covered by a concession contract will be admitted for a concessionaire without a special permit." The Exposition wanted to ward off incidents of "bait and switch" or other behaviors that might deceive or harm the fairgoer.

There were other rules governing behavior on the fairgrounds as well: "Any employee appearing on the grounds intoxicated, making unnecessary noise, or using coarse or insolent language will be deprived of his or her number and be immediately and permanently expelled from the grounds." Concessionaires and their employees were to leave the grounds within two hours after the close of the Exposition, no later than 1:30 a.m.

Some of these contractual agreements were the subject of legal issues and lawsuits with the LPE Co. Chapter 13, "Food Fights and Other Disputes at the Fair," looks at these altercations.

Something for Everyone

Although about one-third of the concessions sold food items, there were many others that met the myriad needs and interests of fairgoers. There were concessions that sold cigars, cigarettes, photographs, guidebooks, cut flowers, perfumes, souvenirs, jewelry, hosiery, postcards and stereoscopic views, suspenders, belt buckles, face creams, crayon portraits, fountain pens, imitation diamonds, window shades, books, shoe polish, and more.

Other concessions sold conveniences, including indoor and outdoor seating, messenger and telegraph services, restrooms, janitorial help, drugstore items, watch repair, dry cleaning, automobile rides, and taxi service.

Food Concessions

The Committee on Concessions had estimated that there would need to be enough eateries to feed about 35,000 people at any given moment, but especially from noon to 2 p.m. and from 5 to 8 p.m.

The Committee on Concessions had estimated that there would need to be enough eateries to feed about 35,000 people at any given moment, but especially from noon to 2 p.m. and from 5 to 8 p.m. They also had to consider a balance of types of restaurants — their size, their prices, and their menus. They needed eateries for those who didn't want to stop and sit for a while ("fast-food" was a term in use at the time of the Fair). People would want snacks for in-between hours. There was also a huge need for caterers who could supply services for the thousands of receptions taking place. These various needs formed a kind of grid, and each food concessionaire was evaluated according to his or her fit in the grid.

The Committee on Concessions granted privileges to concessionaires who provided slot machines for chewing gum and breath wafers as well as to restaurateurs who seated as many as 3,000 people at a time. Some concessionaires got permission to sell candy, soft drinks (1904 style), bottled waters, ice cream, waffles, hamburger and frankfurter sandwiches, chocolate, wine, beer, apple cider, pecans, coffee, tea, maple sugar, and bakery goods.

In High Demand

Most of the time, the committee received one or two applications for a particular food concession. There were nine applicants who sought the rights to sell grape juice and more than 500 applicants who wanted to sell popcorn and peanuts (or "goobers" as they were frequently referred to in 1904). Popcorn and goobers had proven to be a lucrative concession at other world's fairs.

An article in the Dec. 14 1903 *Globe-Democrat* pointed out the obvious about these more popular food snacks: "It doesn't require much capital to get a 450 percent profit return. It needs no financier to prove that anything you can purchase for 1 cent and sell for 5 cents exceeds all the million-dollar businesses in the world. The street candy merchants, popcorn carts, the peanut vendor and banana peddlers are on the way to getting rich. One bunch of bananas and a unfatigued voice will show profits at the end of the day that are all out of proportion to the investment."

By March 1904, the Committee on Concessions had announced the lucky winner of the popcorn and peanut concession: C.A. Windmueller of St. Louis. It was such a big deal that his colleagues held a luncheon to congratulate him on his great fortune. He had so many booths selling popcorn that he had to hire 100 people. Because the electric popcorn popper had yet to be invented, Windmueller met the huge demand by constructing a $10,000 popcorn factory on the Pike. The factory and the concession on the Pike were called "Popcorn Palace," an attractive 40-foot-by-150-foot structure with a large dome and colonnades. Construction finished 10 days before the Fair opened, and Windmueller started popping popcorn right away. Several times a day, his employees filled bags and delivered them to the stands scattered around the fairgrounds.

Fairgoers also loved bananas. Charles Devoto and Company of St. Louis pushed out 16 other applicants for the fruit concession on the Exposition grounds, although he was restricted from selling his fruit in the horticulture or agriculture buildings.

The beverage and restaurant concessions were such an important and profitable aspect of the Fair that you'll learn more about them in Chapter 5, "Everyone Drank at the Fair," and Chapter 6, "The Fare at the Fair."

C.A. Windmueller's popcorn concession included stands like this one at several places on the fairgrounds.

Universal Photo Art Co., courtesy Dr. Lyndon Irwin.

Applications With Clout

Talk about food politics! Sometimes it *is* about who you know. The battle for the orangeade rights is the best example of how competition for a premier concession got sticky. William Knox from Chicago (famous for his gelatin) and A.G. Richardson from Rochester, N.Y., vied for control of the orangeade concession. Orangeade and lemonade came in second to grape juice as the most popular of soft drinks at the time. Knox offered 40 percent of the gross receipts; Richardson proposed a lump sum of $35,000 for 30 locations. The committee decided that Richardson's offer was the best financial choice. However, at the end of Knox's application were the signatures of 20 influential members of the Chicago Press Club — a list too compelling to ignore. Knox was awarded the concession, and he did well by concession standards. His gross income from the Fair was $38,000, of which he turned over $15,178.39 to the LPE Co. But, had they given the concession to Richardson, they would have been $20,000 richer.

Mrs. James Allen Reid, who lived on West Pine, applied for a cafe with retiring and waiting rooms and an afternoon tearoom designed specifically for the rest, comfort, and use of ladies. Her bungalow-style building with 10-foot verandas on each side promised 25 percent to the LPE Co. Professor J.J. Rogers, Chief of the Department of Education at the Fair, had not only referred her, but also proposed that she be given an allotment of space in the Model City section of the Fair. Mrs. Reid's proposal was approved.

Winners and Losers

It is not always obvious from the hundreds of pages of Concession Committee's minutes what the committee members had in mind when accepting and rejecting applicants. Perhaps, after too many hours of meetings, they selected some applications because they were more novel and more fun than others, or because the applicant's proposals just struck the committee's collective fancy.

They approved the Temple of Palmistry, where visitors could have their fortunes read. They also gave the nod to Knute Wideen's bright idea about harnessing the sun's heat with 40,000 mirrors for the lowly purpose of cooking eggs and frying hens. Wideen insisted that, with these mirrors arranged in a manner that he had carefully planned, he could generate any amount of heat up to 10,000 degrees. One applicant caught the attention of the committee when she introduced her new idea: to get products from multiple vendors of small food items — gum, candy, or soft drinks

— and sell them at one cash register. She called it the "Help Yourself Booth." She got the concession, but never showed up at the Fair.

The successful Chicola Manufacturing Co. of St. Louis had its automatic chewing-gum machine application rejected. Although Chicola proposed 30 percent compensation to the LPE Co., the committee denied the request because it simply did not like the design of the machine. Mrs. Reid secured the concession for her ladies' cafe, but H.R. Smith was denied a concession to have his "Gentleman's Buffet" in one of the exhibit palaces.

Concessionaire No. 66 — Sarah Tyson Rorer

When application No. 66 came up for approval, there was little discussion and probably no real need for the applicant to attach glowing testimonials from Exposition Director A.H. Frederick and Senator Dunlap of Illinois. The men on the committee knew the name and reputation of applicant No. 66 — Sarah Tyson Rorer. The committee felt sure that Mrs. Rorer would meet both selection criteria very well — fairgoers would want the opportunity to experience Mrs. Rorer's food and wisdom, and her participation would bring a handsome profit to herself and the LPE Co. They were right on both counts. The committee approved her application and recommended to the executive committee that she be given the concession at the location of her choice — the East Pavilion on Art Hill.

Mrs. Sarah Tyson Rorer in the lower level of her East Pavilion Cafe, where she held cooking demonstrations each weekday afternoon.
Courtesy St. Louis Public Library.

Sarah Tyson Rorer's *World's Fair Souvenir Cook Book* sold for 50 cents plus 7 cents to send it by mail. Every recipe in her book was well thought out and planned with simplicity and health in mind. The rest of the chapters in this book conclude with recipes of Mrs. Rorer's that she might have thought appropriate to "serve" in conjunction with the content or spirit of the chapter. Her recipes draw us back into the turn of the century and give us a taste of what fairgoers might have eaten.

The Fair and the Fairer Sex

"We hear of more women poets, doctors, and authors than ever before. And so it was a confession of inferiority and weakness to huddle the products of women's hands in a building by themselves, as if women were afraid of the comparison with men, as if their work could have no possible chance for award when brought into competition with the work of men," a California newspaper noted about the "place" of women at earlier expositions.

Women architects, sculptors, and painters designed the Women's Building at the Columbian Fair in Chicago, 1893. Women owned and operated the two cafes located at each end of the building's rooftop.

Courtesy Laura Brandt.

St. Louis broke rank from previous fair traditions when it increased the exposure of women's achievement during the 1904 World's Fair. The city always enjoyed when it could "one-up" its Midwest rival, Chicago, and it did just that in front of the whole world in 1904.

At the Chicago Columbian Exposition in 1893, there was one building created to house the work of women's achievements throughout history. The rest of the Fair lionized the achievements of mankind — literally. The Columbian's Board of Lady Managers still managed to display thousands of items made by women, including examples of their art and literature, in the Women's Building. In the basement, two women conducted cooking classes and demonstrations that packed in the crowds each day. Both were grand dames of the art of cookery and directors of their own cooking schools — New York's Juliet Corson and Philadelphia's Sarah Tyson Rorer.

But in St. Louis, women started stepping out of the shadows. Women's ideas for concessions were as welcomed as men's. The farmer's wife put her prized cow next to Farmer Brown's in the Exposition's competition. Equality at the Fair came 16 years before that same farmer's wife would have the right to vote.

Think of this time as a sort of "adolescence" for women: They were somewhere between the weaker sex and the "watch-out" sex. Not that there weren't a few tussles. Exposition leadership waxed and waned on welcoming women's influence at the Fair.

Board of Lady Managers

The Board of Lady Managers was composed of St. Louis socialites. Their daughters would be the future Veiled Prophet queens — the debutantes of St. Louis high society's annual charity event. With few exceptions, their husbands and fathers were affluent and influential. The Board of Lady Managers' focus was to see that women were well represented at the Fair — at least that was its most immediate agenda.

Some of the men wanted the Board of Lady Managers to do what they thought women did best, put on impressive banquets, luncheons, and receptions. They wanted them to add the feminine touch to the often-frenetic pace of the Fair's operations. They did that and did it well. The Board of Lady Managers sponsored hundreds of dining events during the months of the Fair.

The Board, however, expanded its purpose and took on social and moral issues that would come up during the planning of the Fair. It could claim success for the Fair's Sunday closing regulation and played a major role in shaping the "moral" character of the Pike. Some did not want drinking or smoking allowed anywhere or anytime. They strongly preferred that native peoples wear pants, even going so far as having pants delivered to them free of charge!

The relationships between the LPE Co. and the ladies were both cordial and conflicted. When the women requested that the Hootchie Cootchie be banned from the Fair, President Francis said, "Enough." The popular dance involved what

The Board of Lady Managers was a vibrant and influential force at the 1904 World's Fair. Many receptions were held in this drawing room and in other rooms of the Board of Lady Managers Building near the Administration Building.
Courtesy Max Storm.

modern observers would call a negligible rotation of the pelvis. The Fair's president saw no harm in doing the Hootchie Cootchie on the Pike and ignored their request. Good thing, otherwise Andrew Sterling would not have been able to use the term of endearment, "Tootsie Wootsie," in his "Meet Me in St. Louis"!

Whether the men wanted to admit it or not, the women had a lot to do with getting the money for the Fair. Mrs. Daniel Manning, whose late husband was Secretary of the U.S. Treasury, was president of the Board of Lady Managers. When the LPE requested the loan from Congress for $4.5 million, Mrs. Manning made a trip to Washington to speak to her husband's old friends. The men of the Exposition would soon find out that the ladies would become a formidable presence at the LPE. When Francis received the check, Congress had "attached a string." The Board of Lady Managers had to get $100,000 of the loan, which they could spend without any stipulation or restriction on the part of LPE Co. If the company didn't comply, Congress would restrict the loan.

Feminine Appeal

The N.K. Fairbank Co. hired this young woman to represent its very attractive booth in the Palace of Agriculture.
Official World's Fair Photographic Co., courtesy Max Storm.

To say that feminine sex appeal was a primary marketing strategy would be overstated — well, almost. The men who ran the exhibits — especially the food exhibits — recognized the value of attractive women in getting the attention of fairgoers. Like modern airlines 50 years later, exhibitors had specific requirements for a woman's appearance before making her a candidate for hire.

Concessionaires wanted attractive women to staff their booths, serve in their eating establishments, and distribute literature about their food products, and they found them via ads in the newspapers. This ad appeared in the *Globe-Democrat* on April 8, 1904: "Some very attractive ladies are wanted by the Postum Co. Ltd. of Battle Creek, Michigan, for their exhibit of Grape Nuts and Postum Food Coffee at the World's Fair. The successful applicant must possess a handsome face, robust complexion, stylish figure and weigh between 140-165 pounds, and is of pleasing address. Good salaries will be paid." Today, a potential lawsuit, but in 1904 it made perfect business sense.

Either the fairer sex wasn't forthcoming or the bar was set too high because the *Republic* ran an article under the headline "Pretty Girls in Demand." "The competition for pretty girls has reached a critical stage according to the concessionaires and proprietors at the Fair. Despite the enormous supply, the managers here are having much difficulty in filling the places they have at their disposal. Captain Boynton of the 'Shoot the Chutes' show wants four girls to act as ticket sellers for the 'Fairyland' show and is having a great deal of trouble in getting suitable persons. They want girls 18 years old and insist they be uncommonly pretty."

This obsession with beauty may have backfired on the Steinwender-Stoffregen Coffee Co., the maker of Yale Coffee, which also wanted pretty girls to distribute free cups of its coffee to visitors at its exhibit. The Oct. 10, 1904, issue of the *Kansas City Times* reported that the company's turnover of employees was getting to be a problem. Six of their "pretty girl" coffee distributors married men they met at the booths. On an average of one every 20 days, a woman left to permanently fix one man his daily cup of coffee!

A Watchful Eye

Many of the food companies and state exhibitors were selective and protective of young women exhibitors and employees, however. The August 1904 issue of the *World's Fair Bulletin* reported this situation at the Vermont Building: "Young girls dressed in Martha Washington costumes served New England meals. They were young college girls or schoolteachers. Mrs. Boston, the proprietor, is a highly cultured lady who has contained this system of catering from a philanthropic, as well as a business standpoint. Among the young women of her force, she is 'mother' and, although many of the young school-marms have reached the age of discretion, a supervising eye is always upon them, an arrangement which they appear to appreciate."

This same kind of protectiveness was provided when young women from Texas distributed apples on its Apple Day. The girls were assigned official chaperones, both a man and a woman, to ensure the girls' security.

A Growing Field for Women

Throughout most of history, women have done the majority of the food preparation in most cultures. Mothers have taught daughters, and women have shared with each other the secrets of the kitchen.

The formal cooking school was a kind of "going public." It was a late 19th-century concept and became the purview of the American woman. Mary L. Lincoln, Juliet Corson, Catherine Beecher, and Fannie Merritt Farmer were some of the first culinary teachers. The Boston Cooking School, like the cooking schools that followed, offered private classes, public demonstrations, lectures, and special lessons, as well as classes in physiology, psychology, chemistry, and bacteriology.

Graduates went on to teach, direct food programs in schools, direct departments of dietetics in hospitals, give food demonstrations, develop catering businesses, start their own food establishments, write cookbooks, and review cookbooks in national newspapers and journals.

Cookbooks became more scientific in the early 1900s. Ingredients were listed in specific measurements like cups and tablespoons instead of "a piece of butter the size of an egg." With the purchase of gas and electric stoves still not in the budget for many home cooks, exact temperatures were left out of many recipes. Mrs. Rorer's *World's Fair Souvenir Cook Book* often instructed the cook to "put something in or on the fire."

These women were artists whose palettes were the wide range of food available to them, and their judges were the human eye and the human palate. All aspects of food preparation and presentation were experienced in their classes, and table setting was as important as preparing the clearest broth for consommé.

The "Fairest of Them All"

Cooking was now a domestic science with all the analysis, experimentation, authorship, and pedagogy of any proper science. The Fair had the great fortune of having a woman who excelled in all these aspects of domestic science. She had earned the title of the "Nation's Instructress of Dietetics and Cookery." She was Concessionaire No. 66, Sarah Tyson Rorer.

"Many of the ladies enjoy going to Mrs. Rorer's [restaurant] in the east wing of Peristiles Near Festival Hall," reported George Hazen in the *Portland Journal*. In her article, "From a Woman's Standpoint," Countess de Montague informed readers of the *Macon (Ga.) Telegraph*: "Mrs. Sarah Tyson Rorer of cookery-book fame will open a restaurant where food will be prepared on hygienic principles. During the

interlude between the meals this accomplished authority will lecture on domestic economy. In this day of scarcity of domestic help these talks will no doubt prove of inestimable value to young and inexperienced housekeepers." There was rarely a need to explain her identity in any publication, because Mrs. Rorer had the enviable position for any entrepreneur — instant name recognition.

She was no stranger to the exposition scene. The Board of the Chicago World's Fair had commissioned her to demonstrate the many ways to cook corn. Although she had just moved her Philadelphia Cooking School into a free-standing structure a few months earlier, she came to Chicago in 1893 and set up her "corn kitchen" in the basement of the Women's Building. She approached this project in true "Rorer style," which meant that she wrote a pamphlet called the *Recipes Used in Illinois Corn Exhibit Model Kitchen*. It described the many uses of corn and included recipes. She demonstrated the economical uses of corn as well as a way to turn grits into *haute cuisine*. She was not satisfied with just doing her two-hour corn demonstration each day, so she offered month-long classes in all forms of cookery in her "free" afternoons. By the end of the Exposition, 225,000 people had visited Mrs. Rorer's "corn kitchen," and 250,000 of her booklets had gone home to kitchens around the world.

To understand why visitors were excited that Mrs. Rorer was on the fairgrounds and to appreciate her influence at the Exposition, it is important to explain the full

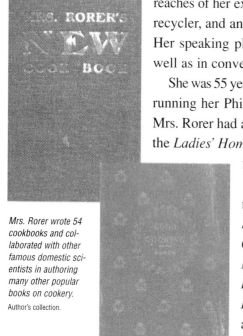

reaches of her expertise. She was a dietitian, a cook, a hygienist, a recycler, and an author. Most of all, however, she was a teacher. Her speaking platforms were in basements and universities, as well as in convention halls.

She was 55 years old when she came to St. Louis, and she had been running her Philadelphia School of Cooking for over 20 years. Mrs. Rorer had also been writing the domestic science column of the *Ladies' Home Journal* for seven years and answering letters from readers about their culinary concerns.

Some of Mrs. Rorer's cookbooks were general references, such as her first classic, *Mrs. Rorer's Philadelphia Cook Book*, and, later, *Mrs. Rorer's New Cook Book*. She wrote cookbooks on specialties, such as *Mrs. Rorer's Everyday Menu Cook Book, Hot Weather Dishes, Home Candy Making, Dainties, Canning and Preserving,* and her two personal favorites, *Chafing Dishes* and *Leftovers*. She authored articles and books well into her 80s.

Mrs. Rorer wrote 54 cookbooks and collaborated with other famous domestic scientists in authoring many other popular books on cookery.
Author's collection.

Some call her the Betty Crocker of 1904, but the likeness cannot be substantiated. Even though "Betty" answered tough questions sent in by readers, she was make-believe. Betty Crocker was the clever marketing idea of CEO William Crocker, who proposed that adding the most popular female name at the time to his surname would give a homey touch to the company's responses to letters about its pie crust. Her "picture" cinched the image.

As a serious dietitian, Mrs. Rorer would have openly frowned on men and women eating too many of Betty Crocker's pies. *The St. Joseph (Mo.) Daily News* reported that in one of her lectures, she said: "Pie is not served on my table at home over three times a year. Pie is the foundation of dyspepsia. Persons with sedentary habits should avoid pie as a plague." Then she turned and demonstrated how to make a really good pie for those times a cook would want to serve it.

Mrs. Rorer did not mince words as she might food for her table. Her reputation for being blunt came to her honestly. About women, she said: "I believe that woman's work is in the house … I believe that work outside is so disagreeable and unpleasant that the Lord saved it for the men to do. Let them have it."

Although men came to Mrs. Rorer's classes and demonstrations, women constituted her largest following. She lectured to women of means, their domestics, and to ordinary housewives. For the seven months of the Fair, she fed the hungry bodies good food in her restaurant, and she fed the minds of those who attended her daily classes. She was indeed the "Fairest of the Fair Sex at the Fair."

Here are some "feminine" recipes from Sarah Tyson Rorer's *World's Fair Souvenir Cook Book*, tasty enough to please the palates of both genders.

Grandmother's Rice Pudding

"Add two tablespoonfuls of washed rice to a quart of milk; add twenty-five raisins, two tablespoonfuls of sugar and a quarter of nutmeg, grated. Stand the basin on the back part of the stove or range, where there is no danger of the milk boiling, and cook for one hour stirring every ten minutes. By this time the rice should be swollen and tender. Now stand in the oven and bake until a nice brown crust is formed. Serve icy cold."

Queen Fritters

"Put a half-pint of water and two ounces of butter in a saucepan to boil. When boiling throw in four ounces of flour, stir rapidly and continually until it sticks together and forms a ball; take from the fire, give a thorough beating and stand aside to cool. When cold, add one egg without beating, and beat until the mixture is thoroughly amalgamated, then add another egg, beat again, and so on until you have added four eggs. Now give the whole a beating for about a minute. Have ready a kettle of hot lard and drop the mixture by spoonfuls into it, allowing plenty of room as they swell four times their original bulk. They will turn themselves, and must be cooked until they stop popping. Serve hot, dusted with sugar and cinnamon."

Lady Cake

"Beat one pound of butter to a light cream, and add one pound of sugar, beat until very light, then add carefully the well-beaten whites of ten eggs, then stir in one pound of flour mixed with two ounces of corn-starch, add a teaspoonful of baking-powder and a teaspoonful of bitter almond or rose water. Bake in a moderate oven about one hour."

Lady's Cabbage

"Put one quart of chopped white cabbage in a kettle of boiling water, add a teaspoon of salt, and boil twenty minutes, drain, turn into a heated dish, pour over cream sauce, and serve. Delicious. More delicate than cauliflower."

CHAPTER 5

Everyone Drank at the Fair

Those who visited St. Louis in the early 1900s probably left with a bad taste in their mouths! The county's fourth-largest city was competitive with Eastern cities both culturally and commercially, but its water was awful — potable, but barely palatable. Most of America's larger cities struggled with this problem, but the Fair managers were aware that poor water could spoil the party for their 20 million guests.

Water

Fearing the Mississippi River would not be a reliable source of clean water for so many people, the planners made a smart business move. In 1901, well ahead of the game, they hired a consultant to make an informed prediction about their water sources. Unfortunately, Gustav Ham Bach, a geologist from Washington University in St. Louis, confirmed their worst fears: the artesian wells around St. Louis were inadequate for the amount of water that would be required at the Fair. Both the public and private sectors were involved in solving this serious problem, and by the time the Fair opened, all types of water were available in abundance. The visitor could obtain pure drinking water in two different ways — for free or for fee!

> The visitor could obtain pure drinking water in two different ways — for free or for fee!

Free-Flowing Water

The city of St. Louis supplied unfiltered water to exhibitors for use with their livestock, fish, or game exhibits. The huge refrigeration plant also received free water because of its immense importance to the functioning of the Fair. In the other exhibits and concessions, the city installed meters and charged 12 cents per 1,000 gallons. Because of continuous complaints of "price gouging," the City Water Co. reduced the cost to 1 cent per 1,000 gallons by July 1904. Visitors drank a filtered version of that water for free, and the LPE Co. footed the bill.

Additional free water was available at bottled-water exhibits in the Agriculture

Building and at the exhibits of water-purifying equipment in the Manufactures Building. The Hygeia Filter Co. and the Standard Water Purifying Co. had working filtration plants at their exhibits and distributed free glasses of their end products during exhibit hours. A visitor could get all the finest purified drinking water he could want free of charge, as long as he didn't get thirsty after 5 p.m.!

Water for a Price

To augment these supplies, the city also granted a contract to the Exposition Water Co., an independent contractor who proposed to transport water from artesian wells in DeSoto, Mo., about 35 miles south of St. Louis. Director of Works, Isaac Taylor, who left nothing to chance, established the purity and potability of that water supply before approving the contract. He had hired doctors Fisk and Cotton, both chemists in St. Louis, to perform bacteriological analyses, and their report gave the water quality the highest of marks. That was good news for the Exposition Water Co., which received one of the largest concessions at the Fair.

The water was transported in railroad cars and stored in tanks on the fairgrounds. During the night, Exposition Water Co. employees filled wagon tanks full of artesian water and drove them to the company's 200 slot machines, located throughout the Exposition grounds. The refrigeration unit connected to the slot device iced the water though the night. Visitors who placed one penny (worth about 20 cents in 2004) in the slot got a squirt of cold, purified water. And on a typical hot St. Louis summer day, that probably hit the spot! The company also made water available for purchase at its booths, but a glass of cold water there cost more than twice as much as it did at the slot machines.

A man from the "Mysterious Asia" attraction, sometimes identified as a "water carrier," satisfies the curiosity and thirst of a visitor to the Pike.
Official Photographic Co., courtesy Max Storm.

A penny in the slot machine produced an ice-cold glass of filtered water for thirsty fairgoers.
Courtesy St. Louis Public Library.

The fairgoer could buy bottled water with familiar labels as well. White Rock, Capitol, American Carlsbad, and Poland Springs advertised, sold, and exhibited their bottled waters at the Exposition. Hotels and restaurants, trying to entice visitors to their establishments, would advertise the brand of bottled water they served.

Unlike most modern water bottlers, however, these companies purported that their waters not only quenched thirst but also improved health. One advertisement for Carlsbad read: "St. Louis is blessed with the privilege of using many waters. Take, for instance, American Carlsbad. It is a natural mineral water and is beyond doubt the best of all foreign and domestic mineral waters. Not only that, but it is the best water for the cure of gout, rheumatism and most efficacious in the cure of stomach and kidney troubles. It is sold by all first-class dealers and the ladies, when they are downtown, can get it at Vaughn's Drug Store opposite the *Post-Dispatch* building. A trial will make you feel like a new person."

Soft Drinks

Say the words "soft drink" after the year 1950 and most people respond: "Coke, Pepsi, 7UP" — the carbonated sodas. Say the same thing before 1950, and a very different list would have emerged — orangeade, grape juice, lemonade, and apple cider. Those were the beverages of choice at the Fair in St. Louis.

Welch's Grape Juice Co., like many companies, promoted its products with unusual giveaways.
Courtesy Max Storm.

Fruit Drinks

A visitor could find fruit drinks on sale everywhere — from the smallest lunch pagoda to the finest of restaurants. A concessionaire as famous as William Knox selling his own brand of orangeade and a "mom-and-pop" concession selling its homemade cider brew could both stand to make a ripe profit in fruit drinks.

Although grape juice is nearly synonymous with Welch's today, this was not true for the 1904 visitor. An investment in the drink by any company rarely went sour. Randall Grape Juice, Malto-Grapo, Gleason Grape Juice, Chautauqua

Fruit, and Welch's Grape Juice were the lucky winners for concession rights at the Fair, and they all set up booths throughout the grounds and exhibit buildings to sell the unfermented drink. Randall Grape Juice from Ripley, N.Y., did so well during the early months of the Fair that it set up a new office at 408 S. Seventh St. in St. Louis, "in order to make more quick and prompt delivery to their patrons."

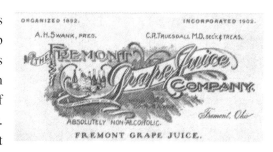

The Welch's Grape Juice Co. established a striking presence at the Fair. Unlike the other companies, Welch's built a prominent two-story building for its employees — on the Pike, no less. Visitors could buy their grape juice and early 20th-century entrepreneurs could witness a model of good business.

Sodas

For such a simple word, "soda" can generate a lot of confusion. To the 1904 fairgoer, "soda" or "soda water" meant one of three things — unflavored carbonated water, flavored carbonated water, or a patented flavored carbonated water! Soda water was water with bubbles — carbon dioxide — infused into it, and the process had been around for 200 years before the World's Fair. Flavored waters were created by adding vanilla, sarsaparilla, chocolate, or any other syrupy concoction to the carbonated water. The commercial soda fountain had popularized these drinks a full century before the Fair.

Patented flavored sodas that existed in 1904 and were known nationally would make a very short list: Coca-Cola, Hires root beer, Moxie, and various brands of ginger ale. Pepsi was not patented until 1905, and neither it nor Moxie had any presence at the Fair. Dr Pepper was a regional drink that will be discussed in Chapter 10, but Hires root beer and Coca-Cola have stories to be told, one simple and one complex.

Hires root beer was very familiar to World's Fair visitors. It was sold throughout the fairgrounds.

Courtesy Max Storm.

Hires root beer is the easy one. The Committee on Concessions granted the rights to sell Hires root beer to Mr. De Long and Mr. Von Boston of Clayton, Mo. There were no "take-home packs" of bottled Hires; those were not invented until the 1920s. Most Hires root beer was sold at soda fountains or booths by the glass. The concession grossed $10,000 and turned $4,000 over to the LPE Co. End of story.

Was the "Real Thing" at the Fair or not? No and yes. In 1903, an application came before the committee from a Coca-Cola bottler in St. Louis. The minutes do not record a specific applicant, but the ante offered for a concession was significant — more than the required 25 percent. "Applications of the St. Louis Cocoa Cola Bottling Co. for concession to sell and manufacture cocoa cola in bottles in five booths in buildings and five stands on the grounds and offering the Exposition 40 percent of the gross receipts as compensation was [were] presented and considered." It would seem to be an offer they could not refuse. But the minutes continue: "The Committee voted to pass [on] the application as from the limited information at hand concerning this drink, it was not deemed wise to grant a concession for its sale."

Coca-Cola had been patented in 1885. Its ingredients are thought to have included a small amount of cocaine and a significant amount of caffeine. By 1903 the use of cocaine was controversial and Coca-Cola decided to use only "spent" cocoa leaves. It also stopped advertising Coca-Cola as a "cure for headaches and other ills." Although the minutes do not state clearly what "limited information at hand concerning this drink," meant, it is reasonable to conclude that the objection centered on the ingredients of the patented formula.

That did not mean the drink was banned from sale in restaurants or at soda fountains. The Louisiana and Texas Rice Kitchen, for example, did not have it printed on its menu, but a copy of that menu in the Missouri Historical Society Collection has "Coca-Cola" written in as part of its beverage offerings. In addition, the

Olympics, which were held at the same time as the Fair and were also sponsored by the LPE Co., advertised and sold Coca-Cola at its events.

Beer

If the Women's Christian Temperance Union had had its way, the Fair would have been dry — or at least semi-dry. But the Exposition leaders knew that temperance would significantly temper proceeds. Ultimately, hotels and restaurants could sell liquor if they fully complied with federal and state regulations, as well the LPE Co. rules. Bottled and draught beer (as well as wine by the glass or by the bottle) appeared on menus throughout the Fair and flowed freely at the thousands of dinners and banquets held during the months of the Fair.

Little wonder that beer was so popular, because St. Louis was the home of

Restaurants often sold one brand of beer exclusively. The Bohemia sold a St. Louis favorite.

Official Photographic Co., courtesy Missouri Historical Society, St. Louis.

45

The Most Popular Brewery in the World.

The Feature of the Louisiana Purchase Exposition
— ST. LOUIS, U. S. A.—

ANHEUSER-BUSCH BREWING ASS'N.

Its Products are used by the Civilized Nations at All Points of the Globe.

An Anheuser-Busch ad in the World's Fair Bulletin, 1904.
Courtesy Max Storm.

Anheuser-Busch and the famous Lemp breweries. In fact, St. Louis had 40 breweries at the time, and many of them contributed to the financial success of the 1904 World's Fair.

August Busch's flagship beer, Budweiser, appeared on many Fair menus, especially the Tyrolean Alps Restaurant in which he was a stockholder. The brew took most of the top juried events. Even one hundred years later, a visitor to the Anheuser-Busch brewery will still find displays of first-place awards from the 1904 Fair.

St. Louis breweries did not have a monopoly on beer, however, despite their strong influence and successful history. Other brewers made a showing, including "the beer that made Milwaukee famous" — Schlitz. The company's ad in the *World's Work Advertiser* appealed to the fairgoer's desire for health and well-being:

The Waukesha Brewing Co., like many of the breweries, advertised the health benefits of beer.
Official Photographic Co., courtesy Missouri Historical Society, St. Louis.

"When tired and exhausted from sightseeing,
you will find nothing more reviving and refreshing than 'Schlitz.'
When the nerves need food, beer is the usual prescription.
So in insomnia; so in nervousness.
The doctor knows that malt and hops are nerve foods and tonic.
He knows that pure beer is good for you. That's why he says 'Schlitz.' "

Coffee and Tea

Coffee and tea appeared on every menu and were equally accessible to the fairgoer on foot. The Lipton Tea Co., the Ceylon Tea Co., and the India Tea Co. sold tea by the cup and in packages to take home. Blanke Foust Blend Coffee, Steinwender-Stoffregen Coffee Co. (the maker of Yale Coffee), and the C.D. Gregg Tea and Coffee Co. all premiered their brews at the Fair. Coffee and tea were listed hot and sometimes iced on most menus. The full story of iced tea can be found in Chapter 10.

The Blanke Coffee and Tea Co. had many small lunchrooms throughout the Fair. This one next to the Pike amusement, "Here-After," served a lot of weary visitors coffee and tea.

Courtesy Max Storm.

"CEYLON" GOVERNMENT BUILDING.
TISSERA'S CEYLON TEAS UNEXCELLED IN QUALITY

Companies took existing postcards and turned them into advertising pieces.

Courtesy Max Storm.

INDIA AND CEYLON TEA PAVILIONS

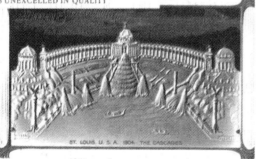

Sarah Tyson Rorer

Fairgoers often checked with each other about the location of a good meal or a good place to get refreshments. "Where can you get a good cup of coffee?" someone might ask.

On May 31, a writer for the *Carthage Missouri Press* commented, "People here are something like a tramp, who is supposed to report to his fellow tramps how he fared at each house, every one is curious to know where you ate and what you paid that he may avoid your pitfalls and profit from your good fortune. Coffee is uniformly ten cents and bad," he said. "Mrs. Rorer, I believe has the only good coffee on the place, and hers is only 15 cents." (That 15 cents today would be $3 — the cost of a cafe latté or cappuccino.)

In addition to everything else for which she was known, Sarah Tyson Rorer was gaining a reputation as a coffee brewer. By 1907, she had her own brand of coffee. Having been inspired by a coffee that she experienced while a juror (perhaps in St. Louis), she managed to find the right roaster, the Climax Coffee and Baking Powder Co., which would produce her coffee and package it with her signature

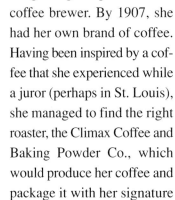

and picture on the bag. The journals that carried her articles also advertised her coffee and encouraged the reader to send in for a free copy of her "27 Coffee Recipes."

Here are some of Sarah Tyson Rorer's drink recipes from the *World's Fair Souvenir Cook Book*:

Coffee

"As there is nothing easier than coffee making, it is a wonder how marvelously bad it is usually done. A little pains, good coffee, and freshly boiled water, is all that is necessary. The first and most important point is the knowing how to select coffee. The best results are usually obtained from a mixture of two-thirds Java, and one-third Mocha … Having settled the choice of coffee, the second important point is the water, which should be freshly boiled soft water … fresh, cold water, brought quickly to a boil, and used at once."

Plain Lemonade

"Pare two lemons and remove all the white skin, then cut them into very thin slices, pour over them a pint of boiling water, and stand aside to cool. When cool, press the lemons, sweeten, and serve with cracked ice."

Blackberry Cordial

"Select the largest and ripest blackberries, mash them and strain them through a flannel. To each quart of this juice allow one pound of granulated sugar, put them in a granite boiler, add a half-ounce of whole cloves, and a quarter of an ounce of stick cinnamon, boil the whole for a few moments until it forms a thin jelly. Take it from the fire, and stand aside to cool. When cold, to each quart add a half-pint of a good brandy. Bottle and seal for use."

Iced Coffee

"Boil twelve ounces of sugar and one pint of water until it forms thickish syrup, then add one pint of strong coffee, which should be made from a blended coffee of Mocha and Java. Scald one quart of cream in a farina boiler, then add it to the syrup and coffee, and when cold, freeze. Serve in glasses."

The Fare at the Fair

Whether it was a craving for Chateaubriand or chicken salad on whole wheat, every fairgoer could find satisfaction on some bill of fare at the Fair. There were about 130 fully staffed eateries on the fairgrounds. In March 1904, the *Republic* reported that there were 25,000 union and nonunion waiters, cooks, chefs, porters, and bartenders already employed by the food concessionaires. Everything was ready. It remained only for the fairgoers to arrive and begin asking the questions, "What to eat?" and "Where to eat?"

The Incubator Cafe was located next to one of the most popular and curious attractions on the Pike. Courtesy Max Storm.

Cooking with gas and electricity were still new to the visitor to the Palace of Electricity. Visitors could purchase food at the Electric Kitchen Cafe after watching demonstrations of these new technologies.

Courtesy Max Storm

Places to Eat

Hungry visitors had many choices to make: What price range? Size and ambiance? Which cuisine? Which brand of coffee? Which label of bottled water? Other patrons? Dress code? Music? Entertainment? Distance to walk? Any combination of answers to these questions could easily be satisfied by the great variety of eateries at the Fair.

Restaurants and Cafes

The restaurants and cafes were usually stand-alone buildings built for the purpose of serving food to seated guests. At these establishments, a diner could sit, see a full menu, be served by a waiter, and sometimes listen to music. Some restaurants had themes like the New England Kitchen or the Dixie Kitchen;

some had unusual sponsors like the House of Hoo Hoo for the Fraternal Order of Lumber Men; and others were in unusual locations like the Incubator Cafe, next to the Incubator Exhibit on the Pike.

Lunch Pagodas

These eateries were also stand-alone buildings, but with little or no seating. Lunch pagodas were the "fast-food" options of the Fair, usually selling hot or cold sandwiches, sides, and drinks.

Lunchrooms

The lunchrooms were welcome finds for fairgoers who had just spent hours looking at exhibits in the palaces. The lunchrooms could often be found in the palaces themselves or in state buildings. Although they seated smaller groups of people and only offered very limited menus, they provided enough refreshment to revitalize the weariest fairgoer for his or her next round of "doing the Exposition."

This lunchroom was located in the central nave in the Palace of Agriculture next to the Quaker Oats Co.'s puffed rice exhibit (detail).

Official Photographic Co., courtesy Missouri Historical Society, St. Louis.

Lunchrooms could be sponsored by the Concessionaires Association or companies exhibiting in the palaces, but sometimes trade associations established lunchrooms for their visiting members. For example, Mrs. Lillie Gregory created the Ranch Club, providing rest, food, and entertainment for rancher men and women visiting the Fair.

Rest Spots

The Board of Lady Managers was apparently thinking about brown-baggers and litterers when its members appeared before the Committee on Concessions to request the right "to establish simple luncheon rooms, where persons bringing their own luncheons can find accommodations, such as tables, etc., plenty of ice-water — possibly the serving of tea, coffee and milk at low rates." They added, "This will tend to good order and prevent the promiscuous scattering of papers, bags, etc. around the grounds."

Other rest spots were stations where visitors could sit and watch people parading by while drinking a hot or cold beverage and perhaps enjoying a doughnut or other pastry. They did not have kitchens for the most part. The Ceylonese, Indian, and Japanese tea houses were the most popular. Their Eastern influence offered peace and quiet after the information overload of the exhibits. One strong advocate for rest spots wrote about the Ceylon Tea House: "Nothing else but [tea and] tea cakes is sold there. In an easy armchair, drawn to a table on the verandas, with the long amber drink before you, do not be in a hurry to leave. There is no smell of the kitchen. Drink another glass of tea, and let the crowd pass on."

Food Booths

These booths peppered the fairgrounds. Similar to kiosks in today's shopping malls and airports, concessionaires generally sold one type of product: soft drinks, candy, chewing gum, fruit, popcorn and peanuts, or coffee and tea.

The Barbecue No. 2 was near the Japanese Pavilion. The Barbeque No. 1 was a few yards from the Ferris Wheel.

Official Photographic Co., courtesy Missouri Historical Society, St. Louis.

Restaurant Guide

The June 1904 issue of the *World's Fair Bulletin* attempted to help Exposition visitors make informed choices about what to eat by printing typical prices from bills of fare at St. Louis restaurants. The publication offered three categories: "Meals at 10 and 20 Cents," "Meals of Moderate Price," and, in the exact words of the *Bulletin*, meals at "One of the Swellest" restaurants. Visitors could use these categories to judge the dining opportunities available on the fairgrounds or the Pike.

Patrons of the Barbecue received an extra bonus with their lunch — a detailed map of the fairgrounds. Of course, the map highlighted the locations of all six Barbecues.

Courtesy Mike Truax.

Meals at 10 and 20 Cents

Concessionaires who financed restaurant buildings and paid chefs, wait staff, and bartenders would not have been able to turn a profit with menu prices this low. If a fairgoer wanted to cut meal expenses, he or she did best to go to one of the lunch pagodas or lunchrooms, where operating costs were lower and savings could be passed on to the customer.

For example, the Universal Lunch Co. of St. Louis managed one of the most popular lunch pagodas. The company had been issued six choice locations, near the Ferris Wheel and the Japanese Tea Garden, for example. Even at a distance, fair visitors could recognize their flag flying above the pagoda roof — "The Flag of the Red Steer." Their specially flavored hot roast beef sandwiches cost 10 cents, homemade pork and beans cost 20 cents, doughnuts as well as their signature Neapolitan ice cream cost a dime. "Nothing over 20 cents," their ads said.

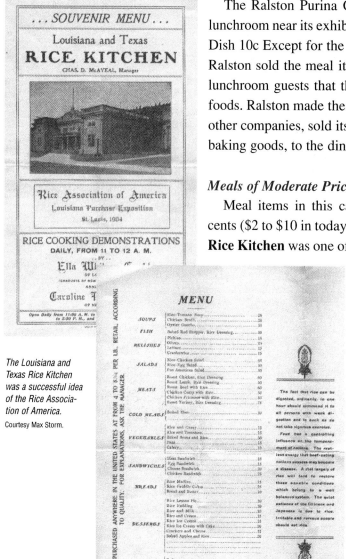

The Louisiana and Texas Rice Kitchen was a successful idea of the Rice Association of America.
Courtesy Max Storm.

The Ralston Purina Co. of St. Louis hosted a low-priced lunchroom near its exhibit in the Palace of Agriculture. "Every Dish 10c Except for the 'Specials,'" the company advertised. Ralston sold the meal items cheaply, but impressed upon the lunchroom guests that the ingredients were pure and healthy foods. Ralston made the food from its own products, and, like other companies, sold its own product line, in this case Purina baking goods, to the diner or visitor right in the lunchroom.

Meals of Moderate Price

Meal items in this category ranged from 10 cents to 50 cents ($2 to $10 in today's market). The **Louisiana and Texas Rice Kitchen** was one of the most popular spots because of its attractive appearance and its location on the Pike. It was often so crowded that there was nowhere to sit, and a waiting line tested the patience of visitors who had already stood in too many queues. Prices were moderate, but the menu stipulated the bottom line: "No order served for less than 25 cents." Boiled rice as well as bread and butter were complimentary with all meat orders of beef, lamb, chicken, or fish. Even the breads and desserts were made from rice. The menu was a souvenir and included instructions for boiling rice properly as well as recipes for rice muffins and rice lemon pie. As you might imagine, the Rice Association of America had financed the entire

At Voney's Quick Meal Restaurant, a fairgoer could sit awhile and enjoy a meal or get a specially prepared carryout lunch.

Courtesy St. Louis Public Library.

operation in order to create an interest in rice grown in Louisiana and Texas.

Voney's Quick Meal Restaurant, moderately priced eatery, provided a double service to the fairgoers. Not only did it offer regular sit-down meals, but it also prepared lunches for patrons who wished to keep on the go. For their convenience, it even packed them in lunch pails that doubled as souvenirs!

The **Inside Inn** was the only concession on the fairgrounds that offered lodging for visitors. Even though it was a swanky hotel, the restaurant prices were moderate. The inn was built by hotelier E.M.

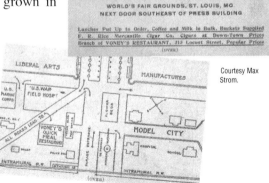

Courtesy Max Strom.

Statler, who is credited with coining the phrase, "The customer is always right." It employed about 2,000 people to care for the thousands of guests who occupied its 2,257 rooms. His Inside Inn at the 1901 Pan-American Fair in Buffalo had made a dismal profit, but he could not resist the invitation to try again in St. Louis.

The inn had two places to eat: a buffet and a restaurant with a total seating capacity of 2,500. Both served food a la carte and kept the cost down. Breakfast and lunch tabs usually amounted to 50 cents, and dinner was priced at about 75 cents.

The hotel was so massive that some rooms were about a mile from the front desk. Statler had chairs put at the end of each guest-room hallway for the bellboys to sit, and one of their jobs was to watch for a wooden arm coming down from the transom of a guest room. This signaled for him to get ice water for the residents of the room — a step toward the concept of room service!

Despite some unexpected problems with serious graft by the wait staff and a huge coffee urn that exploded, injuring Statler and two of his employees, the hotelier ran a first-class establishment. He won high praise from *Collier's Weekly*: "The Inside Inn is a constant joy. It is not entered on the list of exhibits, but of all the shows at the fair, it is the most entertaining and extraordinary."

Dining at Mrs. McCready's American Inn was a treat for those who liked fine dining in a quiet atmosphere. Her restaurant was also known as the Model Restaurant.

Courtesy Max Storm.

"Swellest" Restaurants

Visitors accustomed to fine dining were in for a treat at the Fair. Wealthy patrons who experienced the best foods at home and in the finest dining cars on their way to the Fair would not miss a beat once they arrived at their destination.

The **American Inn** was a restaurant on the cusp of "high-moderate" and "low-swellest." It was also called the Model Restaurant because — you guessed it — it was on the Model Street! Mrs. J.T. McCready, a veteran restaurant owner from the Pan-American Fair, had planned every detail to make the American Inn just as successful. Not only was the good food a draw for fairgoers, but the oversized windows were screened for the visitors' comfort on hot summer days. Some may have been attracted to the inn because the owners had chosen not to sell liquor.

The June 1904 issue of the *World's Fair Bulletin* described the American Inn: "Home cooking, that real home cooking so often heard of, so seldom found, snowy linen, delicate china, glass and plates, excellent service and absolutely 'spick and span' cleanliness in every aspect … complete[s] the model which was aimed at and achieved by Mrs. and Mr. McCready." In addition to her work at the inn, Mrs. McCready was also one of the caterers who supplied refreshments and banquets in state and government pavilions all over the fairgrounds.

The **Palm Cottage Restaurant and Buffet** was one of the more beautiful restaurants on the fairgrounds. It had an excellent location

The Palm Cottage Restaurant offered one of the more unusual forms of entertainment. Diners watched the reenactment of General De Wet's daring escape during the Boer War. A stuntman and his horse dove 35 feet into the water tank.
Official Photographic Co., courtesy Laura Brandt.

at one of the intramural train station stops and was opposite the very popular South African Boer War Exhibit. The exhibit was actually a continuous reenactment of the recent conflict between the British and the Boers, who were South African descendants of Dutch colonists. During dinner, the visitor could witness highlights from the war that were meant to teach and entertain. The reenactment premiered in America at the Fair, and featured a dramatic event diners would be sure to remember: A single Boer soldier on horseback was trapped by a unit of British soldiers. In a desperate effort to save himself, he jumped off a cliff into a stream below. Diners saw the actor dive from a 35-foot-high stand on horseback into a huge vat of water!

The Tyrolean Alps Restaurant could seat more than 5,000 diners at one time at its inside dining hall and its popular outside veranda. Musical groups peformed for diners in both venues.

Lower right, detail of Tyrolean Alps' outside.

The restaurant's literature described The Palm as the "most comfortable restaurant in the Fair grounds, handsomely furnished and beautifully decorated, always cool and … completely screened." The restaurant claimed to have some of the finest chefs in St. Louis, to serve "everything from a ham sandwich to a fifteen course dinner," and to offer all kinds of domestic and imported wines and liquors." Clearly printed on its menu was something St. Louisans were familiar with: "Budweiser Beer Handled Exclusively."

Among the most expensive places to eat was the **Tyrolean Alps Restaurant**. At the eastern end of the Pike was a German village complete with mountains! It had been inspired by a stockholder's trip to the Alps and his desire to bring them home to St. Louis. It received official approval when the German crown prince visited the Fair on opening day: "This is the crowning point of the Exhibition. I shall often come back to look at the Alps."

Central to this vista was the restaurant conceived by August Busch and the LPE Co., underwritten by prominent German St. Louis stockholders, and fleshed out by two of the experts in the restaurant and catering businesses, Tony Faust of St. Louis and August Luchow of New York. The restaurant had a capacity of 5,000 and could seat 3,000 guests in the main dining room alone. Although the room was 200 feet by 400 feet, there were no pillars to obstruct the view, and diners could experience fully the pleasure of being in a "Bavarian Royal Palace." Those who designed the Tyrolean Alps knew well that dining is a total experience, and that what delights the diner's eye and ear will enhance the delights of the palate. Guests listened to classical music played by a 100-piece orchestra. Electric lights draped the ceilings, and European masterpieces from Tyrolean castles hung on the walls.

In addition to the main dining room, side galleries accommodated private parties for more intimate dining. The Tyrolean Alps boasted one of the largest bars in America,

separate ladies' and gentlemen's cafes, and numerous banquet halls. Outdoor dining was also available. There were verandas and terraces where guests could sip a drink and eat all afternoon.

The restaurant owed much of its success to Chef Edward Greenwald and head-waiter Frank Morra. Greenwald arrived at the Fair six months ahead of the opening to prepare the restaurant. He controlled everything concerning the purchase, preparation, storage, and serving of food, as well as managing a corps of 75 cooks. The kitchen was a magnificent place to work. Along one wall stood a 75-foot-long cook range with six broilers, 18 stockpots, 12 vegetable boilers, and two dishwashing machines. Greenwald employed pastry chefs in the large pastry plant and butchers in his butcher shop, requiring that sausage be made fresh daily. Greenwald wanted every guest at the restaurant to feel that the chef had cooked the meal personally for him or her. Morra hired 400 of the best metropolitan-area waiters and managed the elegant service in the dining rooms and on the terraces.

The menu listed 17 different food categories and 194 food items. Eighty-two wines and champagnes made the wine list, and 11 different beers also were offered. Hors d'oeuvres included sardines, herring, pickles and onions, both real and mock turtle soup, soft-shell crab, bass and trout, and eight different kinds of potatoes. Carnivores could indulge in sausage, chicken, veal, mutton, beef, duckling, squab, and goose. Plover and turkey were popular specials. Diners could order a whole turkey for $3 or chicken potpie for 85 cents.

Fruits and fruit compotes offered the calorie-conscious a sweet

finish to their meals. A whole cantaloupe cost only 50 cents, and the ever-popular stewed prunes were half that price. For those who cast their concerns about their waistlines to the wind, the menu beckoned them to try éclairs, cakes, puddings, ice creams, ices, and German specialties.

For the gentlemen, the meal could be completed with a fine cigar. The Tyrolean Alps menu assured guests that: "The Segars sold in the Tyrolean Alps are from the Waldorf Astoria Segar Company of New York. Accept no Segars unless sealed in paper bags and price stamped on in plain figures."

From the first moment of entering the restaurant to the last after-dining experience, Fair visitors were treated royally. And so it was that the Tyrolean Alps Restaurant earned a magnificent reputation and a legacy in world's fair history.

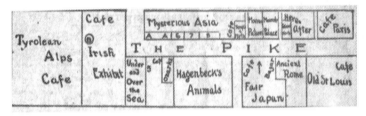

The Daily Official Bulletin *published each day of the Fair mapped out both amusements and eateries on the Pike. The Tyrolean Alps and the international restaurants were two of many eateries spaced out along the mile-long Pike.*
Courtesy Max Storm.

Other "swellest" restaurants at the Fair also had an international flavor. A testimonial in the June issue of *What to Eat* conveyed the experience of eating at another of the Pike's most attractive restaurants: "At the **International Cafe** on the Pike, you don't have to burden your mind with any dietetic problems. Indeed you don't have to think. The thinking is done for you. If you should go to the restaurant, ask for a plate of their spaghetti and you will know what to eat for the rest of your life." Many other national cuisines were also offered at the International Cafe, and, probably more than any other establishment, this restaurant maintained the integrity of the Pike's theme: "To bring the world to the visitors of the Exposition."

Two world-famous caterers and restaurateurs were responsible for the success of the International Cafe: O.B. Abergo and A. Baroni, whose names were famous from the other expositions. But one restaurant in St. Louis was not enough for them; they also operated the **Alexandria Restaurant** in conjunction with the Cairo concession on the Pike. Both restaurants were designed to attract the foreign visitor as well as American fair attendees, and the combined wait staff and other personnel could speak 43 languages! Because most of the buildings on the Exposition grounds (those areas excluding the Pike) closed in early evening, the masses of workers were often free to take dinner on the Pike. These two restaurants turned out to be a kind of "convention center for concessionaires and exhibitors."

Abergo and Baroni selected their surroundings and their chefs to fill their vision of a true international restaurant. They hired special chefs for Italian, Spanish, Mexican, South American, and Oriental dishes. Their head chef had experience at the Hotel Ritz in Paris, the Auditorium in Chicago, and, at the time of the Fair, was working at Delmonico's in New York. Abergo and Baroni partnered with the 50-year-old John Gund Brewing Co. of La Crosse, Wis., to offer a custom-made beer for the Fair that had taken two years to develop. To educate the diners and advance the public relations for the John Gund Brewing Co., company representative R. Walter answered questions about the beer. He was well-prepared for the restaurant's international clientele because he alone spoke 11 languages.

The **German Wine Restaurant** was known to have the finest but most expensive bill of fare. Unprepared visitors like William Maher wrote: "The German Restaurant is a fine building and an attractive situation once you have climbed the 115 steps, and one you turn to with a confident feeling that you will find good things. We went there for a light lunch. The room was well filled and very few tables were unoccupied. We were seated and given ice water, and then the waiter handed us his menu card. The first thing that arrested our attention was a line in large print at the top: 'PRICE FOR LUNCH $2' [$40 by 2004 prices]." Maher went on to reason that, if he had been there with a very big appetite, this was a fine situation, but he had come for a *light* lunch. "Asked if they served nothing but the full $2 lunch, the waiter said they did not." Maher's June 1904 newspaper article, "A Peep at the St. Louis

The German Wine Restaurant was one of the most talked-about restaurants at the Fair. It served excellent food and fine German wines.
Courtesy Louise Drescher.

Fair," might have discouraged some visitors from the German Wine Restaurant, but attracted others whose stomachs or wallets were more ample!

The firm that ran the German Wine Restaurant reported that, "The Kaiser himself had ordered that the service be of the highest German grade in order that a favorable impression be given of German Cooking." In the end, this kind of pressure blew the lid off the company, and, in March 1905, the *Republic* did a follow-up article on the German Wine Restaurant: The losses sustained by the restaurant at the World's Fair had caused the parent company in Berlin to fail also and eventually go out of business.

A delicate and ornately decorated fan was a prize souvenir from the German Wine Restaurant (below).
Courtesy Max Storm.

"Funnest" Restaurants

Waiters dressed like coal miners served diners at the Anthracite Coal Restaurant.
Courtesy Missouri Historical Society, St. Louis.

If the Tyrolean Alps and international restaurants were the "swellest," then there were surely restaurants and cafes that could qualify as the "funnest."

One of these was the **Anthracite Coal Mine Restaurant**, located in the exhibit of the same name. This exhibit informed visitors about every detail of modern coal mining in the anthracite fields of Pennsylvania. Hungry or bored visitors could descend to the restaurant below for a Dutch lunch served by miners in miners' clothes — including hats with lights on them. The walls and floors were made of anthracite coal, and the place was lit with miners' lamps. To further simulate the experience for the visitor, a large fan — like those used to send air through the real mines — kept cool breezes blowing through the lunchroom.

mines — kept cool breezes blowing through the lunchroom.

The **Bird Cage Cafe** was another "fun" spot. It was just outside the giant bird cage, one of the few permanent structures built for the Fair, and currently part of the St. Louis Zoo. From the windows of the cafe, patrons could watch Fair visitors walking around the inside of the bird cage as well as almost every species of American birds flying overhead. It was a find for both people watchers and bird-watchers.

Although the Ferris Wheel, the rotating "Observation Wheel" that was a repeat attraction from the Chicago World's Fair, was not an "official" food concession, it quickly became the scene of some of the "funnest" eating events. Plans for the Ferris Wheel had not included an official dining car among its trolley-sized cars, but, by July 1904, so many banquets and celebrations had taken place there that one of the cars was dubbed the **"Ferris Wheel Diner."** "The mere

The Ferris or Observation Wheel became a unique dining experience as the months of the Fair progressed. If that idea was unappealing, a hungry fairgoer could frequent the Swedish Restaurant a short distance away. The marquee says that it served Triscuits.

Official Photographic Co., courtesy Missouri Historical Society, St. Louis.

thought of eating one's soup or ices while moving through the air hundreds of feet above the heads of common mortals, and 150 feet above the highest point of any building on the grounds, arouses a comfortable thrill of expectation," reported the writer for the *National Fruit Grower* journal. An article appearing in the *Globe-Democrat* reported that, "scores of weddings took place [on the Ferris Wheel]. One couple got married on horseback in one of the cars … Cars were rented for an entire evening and tables were set and meals served while the wheel made its circuits." An example of one of these events took place on June 21 at 7 p.m. A group of 60 engineers and inspectors from the World's Fair climbed into car No. 19 to honor G.W. Branchi, the city's boiler inspector. The car was decorated for the occasion, and the group sat around a table eating, drinking, and toasting Branchi. When car No. 19 reached the 250-foot zenith of its ride, Charles Foster, superintendent of the power plant, stood, gave an appropriate speech, and then presented Branchi with a diamond-studded gold watch. The guests could see the lights of the Fair and of the whole city of St. Louis beneath them as they finished their refreshments.

Special-Interest Restaurants

For history buffs, there were many places to visit that allowed them not only the opportunity to go back in time but also to get a decent 1904 meal. The Irish arranged for a walk across imported Irish sod before entering a reproduction of the **Old Irish Parliament** and its restaurant. The **Old St. Louis Restaurant** replicated the ambience of the city's 18th-century beginnings.

Ulysses Grant, Theodore Roosevelt, an unknown Nebraskan, and the poet John

The Blanke Tea and Coffee Co. purchased Grant's Cabin and also secured the concession to sell food from the cabin during the Fair.

Courtesy Max Storm.

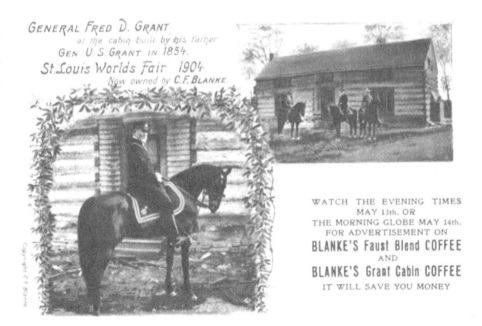

GENERAL FRED D. GRANT
at the cabin built by his father
GEN U.S. GRANT IN 1854.
St. Louis World's Fair 1904
Now owned by C.F. BLANKE.

WATCH THE EVENING TIMES
MAY 13th. OR
THE MORNING GLOBE MAY 14th.
FOR ADVERTISEMENT ON
BLANKE'S Faust Blend COFFEE
AND
BLANKE'S Grant Cabin COFFEE
IT WILL SAVE YOU MONEY

Burns all had something in common: their cabins were brought to the Fair and were open to the history-minded. Although Roosevelt was the only one still among the living, the rest had benefactors to keep their former domiciles "alive and cooking" — at least at the Fair, where the cabins included places to eat that had appropriate menus. For example, the Burns Cottage Association hired a Scottish cook to provide authentic shortbread, oatcakes, currant cakes, scones, and bannocks. Lemonade and Scotch whisky were also for sale.

One of the most unusual special-interest eateries was **Mrs. MacMurphy's Restaurant for Dyspeptics**. In 1904, much attention was given to the various ailments of the stomach, and Harriet MacMurphy of Omaha, Neb., thought it was important to have a restaurant that catered to those who suffered from indigestion. She moved into the building abandoned by Nebraska when it chose to try an alternate way of displaying the advancements of the state, and she set up her restaurant there. When asked what she would serve, she replied, "Well, really I can hardly say just now. You see, I shall prepare these meals with a view to the summer season as well. For instance, there will be fewer meat dishes included on my bill of fare than one would naturally have in winter season. Fruit, yes, lots of cooked fruit and fresh fruit; salads if vegetables are available."

Sarah Tyson Rorer

"At a very handsome building, not far from this [the German Wine Restaurant], Mrs. Rorer, the well-known writer about cookery, has a restaurant and we became pretty regular patrons there, for to our thinking, everything brought on the table was fine in quality, deliciously cooked, and very daintily served" – so commented William Maher in his June 1904 article, "A Peep at the St. Louis Fair."

Sarah Tyson Rorer had never owned or operated a restaurant until she came to the Fair in St. Louis, but she named her newest business venture the "Model Dining Company." Unlike other restaurant owners, Mrs. Rorer did not need to construct a building for her establishment because the Exposition had granted her the right to rent the highly coveted East Pavilion. This was one of the rotundas on either side of Festival Hall, which overlooked the Cascades and the Grand Basin. Even the Tyrolean Alps, with all its size and grandeur, could not compete with the simple elegance of Mrs. Rorer's **East Pavilion Cafe** or Model Cafe.

Just a short walk across Art Hill brought the visitor to the **West Pavilion Restaurant** or the Grand Cascade Restaurant. This was Fair President Francis's private dining room, as well as where the directors served their prominent guests. While all of the Roosevelts ate there in the West Pavilion, most of the fairgoers would have just looked at the building and gone across to the East Pavilion for a cup of coffee at Mrs. Rorer's.

A view of Mrs. Rorer's restaurant from the lagoon.

Official Photographic Co., courtesy Laura Brandt.

Mrs. Rorer rented the East Pavilion for $7,500 for the duration of the Fair, which would be about $20,000 per month in today's money. Businessmen like Maher were quick to realize Mrs. Rorer's investment and had little sympathy with anyone who might complain about the reasonable prices. In his "Peep" newspaper article, he wrote: "I recall a chat I had with Mrs. Rorer's manager: he told me they paid $8 a week to the girls who waited on the tables. As the Fair is not open on Sunday, this is for six days. …Then they pay to the Fair authorities rent and for the privilege of running the restaurant, one quarter of every dollar they take in. Study that for a second and then look at Mrs. Rorer's prices and tell me if you would like to take the contract off her hands. I am mighty sure I would not at one-half the terms."

To ensure that her investment of time and money would be profitable, Mrs. Rorer made the utmost use of the space available to her and squeezed every eating opportunity out of every day. She used the first and second floors for food preparation, and the third floor and roof garden for private dining rooms. There she served noon breakfasts, luncheons, afternoon teas, suppers, chafing-dish meals, and dinners.

Maher wrote about one of her specialties in the "Peep" article: "I noticed that Mrs. Rorer's customers were liberal patronizers of her baked beans and brown bread for 30 cents. The beans were served in the pot in which they were baked and there was enough in one of these to make a hearty meal for a working man." Mrs. Rorer put her Boston Brown Bread recipe in the *World's Fair Souvenir Cook Book* but, for some reason, did not include her famous baked beans! The recipe to the right is taken from her 1902 classic, *Mrs. Rorer's New Cook Book*, pp. 329-330.

Boston Brown Bread

"Put into a large bowl two cups of Yankee rye meal (not rye flour), two cups of coarse Indian meal, and a teaspoonful of salt. Dissolve a teaspoonful of soda in two tablespoonfuls of boiling water, and then add it to one and a half pints of sour milk; add one cup of molasses and pour it on the meal. Beat continuously for about ten minutes, or until all the ingredients are thoroughly mixed. Pour into well-greased moulds, put on the lid and steam for five hours. Then remove the lid, and bake in a moderately quick oven for thirty minutes."

Baked Beans

"Use 1 quart of small white soup beans, 1 pound of salt or pickled pork, and 2 tablespoonfuls of molasses. Soak the beans over night. The next morning, wash them and put them into a kettle of boiling water and boil until the skins will crack when you blow on them. They must not be soft. Score the rind of the pork and boil it with the beans. When the skin of the beans cracks, take them from the fire: drain and turn them at once into the bean pot: bury the pork in the centre until only the scored skin remains above the beans. Put a teaspoonful of salt and the molasses into one pint of the water in which the beans were boiled; mix and pour over the beans in the pot. This should just come to the surface. Put on the lid and bake in a moderate oven from six to eight hours. Add more of the bean water as that in the pot evaporates. If properly done, each bean will be soft; no two beans should stick together. The water will have entirely evaporated and the beans are a dark, rich brown in color. If the beans have been boiled too long they will not keep shape in baking."

Free Lunch at the Fair!

Contrary to the popular saying, "There's no such thing as a free lunch," there actually was a "free lunch" at the Fair, and a free breakfast as well! Free food was served in many state buildings and some palaces, and, if fairgoers were careful about amounts and combinations, they would not automatically end up at Mrs. MacMurphy's Restaurant for Dyspeptics! At no charge, fairgoers could indulge in a late breakfast of Postum cereal, oatmeal, Grape Nuts, biscuits, breads, hot rolls, preserves, doughnuts and coffee, hot cocoa, or tea. They could also catch an early lunch before noon or a late lunch after 2 p.m. that might include samples of salmon salad, pork and beans, pickles, olives, catsup, consommé, canned ham, fudge, cakes, chocolates, milk, buttermilk, ice cream, or gelatin desserts — all received a la carte by visiting various company or state exhibit booths.

> Contrary to the popular saying, "There's no such thing as a free lunch," there actually was a "free lunch" at the Fair, and a free breakfast as well!

Profit and Profit

There were two reasons for the proliferation of free food and the literature that accompanied the edible handouts: profit and profit. The nation's greatest industry in 1904 was agriculture. Both the grower and producer depended on a strong market, and 20 million potential buyers showed up at the Fair. That made it the marketing opportunity of a lifetime.

Companies displayed their finest product lines, hoping to establish brand recognition and customer loyalty. States and countries sent the best of their harvests, hoping to increase commerce to their areas. Western states needed more people and were convinced they could lure more settlers by appealing to their taste buds! Sometimes the smells wafting from the booths were too much for the passersby to resist. Like the sirens of ancient mythology, these food samples drew the crowds to booths where they would be transformed, hopefully, into loyal customers.

Nowhere was free food more lavishly distributed than in the palaces of agriculture and horticulture. These palaces displayed the world's abundance of food and the plethora of products made from it. Both food concession owners and the director of the agriculture and horticulture exhibits were concerned about the predicted amount of free vittles that would be dispersed. Frederic W. Taylor, superintendent of the exhibits, ruled that exhibitors could not dole out free food between the hours of noon and 2:00 p.m. As readers learned in the March 22 issue of the *Post-Dispatch*, "Mr. Taylor is afraid that unless they [the exhibitors] are restricted, the food exhibits will feed the people free and leave no appetites for the people who are paying for restaurant privileges upon the grounds. Mr. Taylor has been moved to this view by the briskness with which the cereal concerns, bread and flour companies etc.

Minnesota's building gave out complimentary servings of pickles, baked beans, and bread and butter each day at lunch.
Courtesy Max Storm.

are making preparations to feed the masses with every breakfast food, cookie, cake, and patented pie ever devised by man."

In addition to the exhibits, there were various other sources of freebies. The German Building gave out free lunches every day, and the Oregon Building offered free lunches for Oregonians. On special days, like Apple Day, train carloads of the fruit were given away.

Baked beans were a favorite American dish in 1904. Van Kamps gave away a lot of its top seller.
Author's collection.

Food Companies

Some of the hundreds of food companies exhibiting at the Fair have had the great fortune of sustaining name brand recognition for more than a century — Van Kamp, Heinz, Jell-O, Welch, Pillsbury, Ralston Purina, Wesson, Baker Chocolate, Log Cabin Syrup, Hires, Anheuser-Busch, and Jack Daniel. Others, like Cottolene, the maker of a well-known lard substitute, and Eskays, famous for its baby foods, closed their doors or merged with other companies during the 20th century.

Because educating the visitor with visual and interactive experiences was both in line with the vision of the Exposition and characteristic of a successful booth, much of the free food was a byproduct of the many presentations that went on all day. Food companies hoped that the demonstrations would engage visitors long enough to convince them that their product was the best of its type. If timed just right, however, the hungry and clever visitor could scoot in and pick up a nice chunk of freshly made chocolate from the Baker Co. exhibit, some pudding from the St. Charles Creamery, or some hot biscuits from the Ralston Purina Co. without even waiting for the demonstration to be over.

D.G. COOK, PREST.

Cook's Imperial EXTRY DRY

WORLD'S FAIR

ST. LOUIS, 1904

EXHIBIT; AGRICULTURAL BLDG SEC. 72

Wine, whiskey, and beer samples were given to those of age at the exhibits in the palaces of agriculture and manufactures.
Courtesy Max Storm.

Even if not as good as Mrs. Rorer's 15-cent coffee, there was plenty of free coffee for the tired fairgoer. Competition for the best "cuppa Jo" was brewing in the Agriculture Building. The Steinwender-Stoffregen Coffee Co. and the Blanke Tea and Coffee Co. sold their coffees in restaurants and at their own concessions throughout the fairgrounds, but their booths at the Agriculture Building served it free. The Brazil exhibit's organizers estimated that they distributed 5,000 free cups of coffee each day while visitors watched their exhibit of a large fountain cascading coffee beans instead of water. Not to be outdone was the Planters Association's exhibit, which distributed free coffee in "dainty cups served by young ladies from the better families in San Juan and Ponce to the quaint strains of the Puerto Rican string orchestra." Less ostentatiously, and probably for good reason, the Jack Daniel distillery gave out miniature samples of its spirits. Other distilleries did likewise, somehow avoiding the radar screen of the Women's Christian Temperance Union.

Take-Home Products

Not all free foods had to be eaten on the spot. Some were packaged to be taken home and to be used or shared, but, above all, they were to be remembered at the next trip to the grocery store. Besides enjoying the variety of fresh, right-out-of-the-oven bread products baked on the premises by the Pillsbury Co., visitors to the company's display in the Palace of Manufactures received a small sack of Pillsbury's Best Flour and a 32-page recipe booklet. The Towles Log Cabin Syrup Co. built a cabin with maple logs and filled it with thousands of cans of its syrup. Everyone got a peek into the reproduction

Towle's Log Cabin maple syrup cans filled almost everyone's Ralston Purina bag.
Courtesy Max Storm.

The Pillsbury-Washburn Co.'s exhibit gave away plenty of baked goods as well as a miniature sack of its Pillsbury's Best Flour.
Official World's Fair Photographic Co., courtesy Missouri Historical Society, St. Louis.

of an early settler cabin, heard the story of Towles syrup, and received a complimentary can.

Heinz brought all its varieties to the Fair, and, like other food companies, tried to appeal to all of the senses — not just to taste. In addition to giving away many edible pickles, it also gave away reproductions of them, e.g., a little pickle pin to wear on one's lapel. Heinz excelled at subtle aspects of marketing, and these pins proved to be the company's most popular giveaway. When men and women were interviewed by this author in 1981 about their experiences at the Fair, all of them recalled that their favorite souvenir was the little pickle pin. In fact, more of them remembered the Heinz giveaway pin than they did the ice cream cone!

Another class of giveaways was the promise of a sample mailed to one's home address. For example, a visitor who had tasted the popular Shoyu seasoning at Fair Japan could write the sponsoring company for a sample.

Giveaways Galore

Hundreds of thousands of pieces of literature accompanied the free food samples. The exhibitors used sound marketing strategies and knew the importance of keeping the product in front of the potential consumer. They were counting on the natural human drive to accumu-

The H.J. Heinz Co.'s booth made quite a showing at the Fair, and its little pickle charm (left) was a hit with children and adults.

Shara (Jessie) Storm, courtesy Max Storm (pickle).

Courtesy H.J. Heinz Co., author's collection.

Except for the cost of postage, the fairgoer could write the company that made the popular Japanese seasoning, Shoyu, and request a free sample.

Courtesy Max Storm.

After consuming free samples of the new flavored gelatins of Jell-O, fairgoers took home complimentary recipe booklets of the "fast-food" product.

Courtesy Max Storm.

late and the wistful desire to receive something for nothing.

When a delegation of Massachusetts editors came back from the Fair, they wrote for the August issue of the *New England Grocer*: "Exhibitors … are distributing literature by the carload daily in the shape of advertising cards, dainty booklets and folders, advertising pieces of all kinds, from pasteboard boxes [referring to the ubiquitous "Purina bag"] suitable as carriers for lunches or souvenirs, to handbags and doilies of linens. [There are] calendars, stickpins of pickles, tiny fish or grain, photographs of babies brought up on proper food, … ivory buttons, celluloid hearts and metal trinkets. [This is] to say nothing of the charts, health talks, menus and recipes, and lastly the 'samples' all of which will lead to far reaching and beneficial results, especially when the sight-seeing housekeeper has time to form her own conclusions after going over her collection at leisure."

Another giveaway required a little more effort. An unidentified newspaper article included in Frederic Taylor's scrapbook reported that an unnamed St. Louis cereal manufacturer had organized a club among the retail grocers who handled his products. About 2,000 members were given sterling silver rings with advertising on them, and, if the members showed that ring at the Fair, they were given free meals at the company's factory. The only initiation fee was an order of five cases of the manufacturer's product, probably not a bad deal for the grocers.

The smell of Baker Chocolate Co.'s confection often wafted through the aisles of the Palace of Agriculture. The company was generous with its samples and its literature.

Courtesy Max Storm.

Healthy Concerns

Perhaps it was a good thing that there were so many miles of aisles in the Agriculture Building, because there were certainly some extra calories to walk off. An unidentified newspaper warned: "As the spectators watch the vast crowds that seem never to satisfy that 'aching void,' almost all of the participants give evidence of indulging in three or four square meals per day, they are made to wonder how many funerals will be the immediate outcome of all this banqueting. The only ray of hope regarding the physical welfare of the habitual free-luncher is the closing of the exposition, which is so near at hand. Still [I] fear that dyspepsia will hold unlimited sway in thousands of cases before the six weeks are ended and it has been suggested that at least two emergency hospitals ought to be established without delay in the immediate vicinity of the free lunch counters."

It might be giving too much credit where credit is not due, but perhaps the Committee on Concessions considered the matter of over-indulgence when it approved the American Talking Scale Co.'s application to place a number of its scales throughout the fairgrounds. The overfed, underfed, or merely curious visitor placed a penny in the slot, stood on the scale, and waited for the trumpet on the scale's automated system to announce his or her correct weight. It is hard to imagine that this would be a popular concession in 2004!

The Concordia Turners, a German gymnastic club that promoted a sound body and a sound mind, sponsored a booth that gave free literature on health and its famous exercise program. On German Day, the Turners demonstrated their system of keeping fit. At least once at the Fair, visitors could observe one way of dealing with the ill effects of too much "free lunching."

Young Turners demonstrated the proper way to do gymnastics and stay fit on German Day at the Fair. Fairgoers who had been experiencing a lot of free lunches were wise to take heed.

Courtesy St. Louis Public Library.

Sarah Tyson Rorer

In between the two meals served in the East Pavilion Cafe, Mrs. Rorer was in her model kitchen demonstrating the recipes printed in the *World's Fair Souvenir Cook Book*. Like cooking classes held at the Kitchen Conservatory today in St. Louis, the food from Mrs. Rorer's demonstrations ended up on the plates of observing students. Her classes provided her reading audience a chance to sit at the feet of the master, taste her works of art, and get a free lunch out of it, too.

Here are some items from Mrs. Rorer's luncheon menu that she might have demonstrated in her Model Kitchen. If she had, fairgoers would have gotten quite a tasty value at their "free lunch."

In the afternoon Mrs. Rorer gave demonstrations in the basement of the East Pavilion. Fairgoers could have used the map on pages 172–173 to find her location.

Author's collection.

Tomato soup: . . . . 20 cents
Broiled chicken with cream sauce, peas, bread, and butter: . . . . 50 cents
Ham sandwich: . . . . 20 cents
Chicken salad sandwich: . . . . 50 cents
Strawberry shortcake and cream: . . . . 40 cents
Shredded wheat with strawberries and cream: . . . . 40 cents
Coffee: . . . . 15 cents
Tea: . . . . 15 cents
Buttermilk: . . . . 15 cents

The following recipes are from Mrs. Rorer's *World's Fair Souvenir Cook Book*, and may inspire some contemporary cooks to prepare free lunches for their friends.

Chicken Salad

"Draw, singe, and gently boil a chicken until tender. When done, and perfectly cold, remove the skin and cut the meat into dice. If you want it very nice, use only the white meat, save the dark for croquettes. After you have cut it, stand it away in a cold place until wanted. Wash and cut the white parts of celery into pieces about a half-inch long, throw them into a bowl of cold water and stand them away until wanted. To every pint of chicken allow two-thirds of a pint of celery, and a cup and a half of mayonnaise dressing. When ready to serve, dry the celery and mix with the chicken, dust lightly with salt, white pepper or cayenne, then mix with it the mayonnaise. Serve on a cold dish garnished with the white celery."

A Good Tomato Soup

"Trim the fat from a slice of ham. Put the ham away for another meal. Cut this fat into pieces and fry with a sliced onion until nicely browned. Turn one can of tomatoes into a stewing-pan, add the browned pieces of ham fat and onion, a teaspoonful of salt and a quarter teaspoonful of pepper, cover and simmer ten minutes. Add two tablespoonfuls of flour to the fat remaining in the pan, which should be a good tablespoonful; if not, add butter, mix until smooth, add it to the tomatoes, stir until they boil, and then press through a sieve; add a teaspoonful of sugar and serve with squares of toasted bread."

Strawberry Cream Cake

"Make a very light sponge cake from six eggs, and bake it in three jelly cake tins. While it is baking and cooling, cover a quarter-box of gelatine with a half-cup of cold water, and soak a half-hour. Whip one pint of cream, and put it in a tin or granite pan; stand this pan in another containing cracked ice, add to the cream a half-cup of powdered sugar and a teaspoonful of vanilla sugar. Stir the gelatine over boiling water until it dissolves, add it to the cream and stir at once, and continue stirring until the cream begins to thicken. When the cakes are cold put over one a thick layer of this cream; then stand strawberries evenly all over it; put on another layer of the cake, cover it with cream and berries, and so continue, having the top layer cream and berries. Serve very cold."

CHAPTER 8

Food for Thought

Grazing for free food at the Fair was not like Saturday afternoon at Sam's Club or Costco, even though the feast of samples was almost endless. Exposition leaders were very clear that no exhibitor was going to benefit from the tremendous opportunities for exposure unless they ultimately taught fairgoers something new.

> "The chief value and purpose of the World's Fair at St. Louis, like that of all expositions of this character, will be educational. Its exhibits must *do* something more than gratify mere idle and thoughtless curiosity."

Already in June 1903, publications like *What to Eat* were telling readers that: "The chief value and purpose of the World's Fair at St. Louis, like that of all expositions of this character, will be educational. Its exhibits must *do* something more than gratify mere idle and thoughtless curiosity." In an early 1904 issue of *Cosmopolitan*, a writer was even more explicit: "Exhibits of confectioners, chocolate makers, soda fountain manufacturers and bakers will be installed at the Fair. These displays will partake of the central idea of the Exposition — life and motion. Moving exhibits are the sought-after things in all departments. Every exhibitor, where practical, is expected to be doing things. This is an age when people 'want to know how.' So the candy maker can show his processes. The chocolate manufacturer can display his methods and results so far as he is willing the public shall know."

The Exhibitors' Response

The food exhibitors responded well to this mandate. A company like Pillsbury-Washburn Mills of Minneapolis did not simply hand out hundreds of thousands of hot biscuits slathered with fresh butter. Part of its exhibit illustrated the wheat-growing, flour-making, and bread-baking processes with detailed photographs, taking the viewer from wheat and chaff to biscuits and cookies.

But the exhibit did even more than that. The *Flour Trader News* was impressed with Pillsbury-Washburn's compliance with the Fair's dictate, reporting in August 1904 that, "… a complete bakeshop with mixing machines, proving troughs, and electrical ovens is provided. Here an opportunity is given to the public to watch the different stages of procedures, which must be passed, before flour can be turned into nourishing bread and which prove a revelation to a good many visitors. A practical baker in a neat white uniform attends to all the technical processes and the visitors sample the finished product."

Like a number of other companies hoping to capture the visitors' hearts and loyalties, Pillsbury-Washburn encouraged them to linger at the display. Visitors could sit comfortably and quietly in the rooftop cafe, purchase tea or coffee to accompany their generous free samples, read their *Pillsbury's Best* recipe book, and enjoy the panoramic view of the enormity of the Agriculture Building.

Most companies followed suit. The Sunnybrook Distillers demonstrated the complete production of its whiskeys, providing an observation point for fairgoers. They saw the how and why of what was inside the bottle and the paper label that sealed it. The U.S. government granted a permit for the operation of the distillery, and the adjoining warehouse became a government-bonded building for handling the product.

The Walter Baker Chocolate Co. had a two-story replica of its company built inside the Agriculture Building with special equipment designed by German engineers. Baker displayed the making of chocolates from cocoa beans to truffles. On the second floor of the building was the kitchen run by a veteran employee who demonstrated candy making. While the smell of pure chocolate wafted through the room, visitors could get samples or buy Baker's vanilla and cocoa chocolate in the exhibit's store.

In every part of the Walter Baker Co.'s booth, there were demonstrations of candy making and state-of-the-art candy-making equipment. On the second floor, patrons sat at small serving tables to enjoy vanilla, chocolate, and cocoa.

Courtesy Dr. Lyndon Irwin.

State and Country Exhibits

Equally active in providing demonstrations for fairgoers were the many state and country exhibits. California's Santa Clara County had one of the most famous displays — prunes — and the county appropriated $500 a month for prune-cooking demonstrations. Believe it or not, at the turn of the century the two most popular fruits were apples and prunes. Santa Clara educated fairgoers on the health benefits of dried fruit and gave away free prunes as well as suggestions for cooking them. The appeal of the prunes was evident because the rationed supply of giveaways was depleted by noon each day. Two other Californians, a Miss McNaugton and a Miss March, showed that flowers could be edible. They demonstrated how to make pink, white, yellow, and red rose petals into candy.

The French built a typical Parisian bakery in the Agriculture Building, and not only provided samples and products for sale, but also supplied a large number of the restaurants on the fairgrounds with their baked goods. The English also established a working bakery in the Agriculture Building and popularized a baked good less familiar to Americans — the scone.

Lending Credibility to the Exhibits

Thousands of people were employed to demonstrate various aspects of food processing. Some companies brought their own employees. For example, Ralston Purina had its millers demonstrating the process of flour production. Others were hired specifically for the Fair, and great care was taken to select people who would create a good impression. Companies wanted physical attractiveness, but were also on the lookout for attractive minds. Pillsbury-Washburn hired a professional woman from the Agriculture Department of the University of Minnesota to demonstrate milling processes. She spoke several languages and had no trouble holding people's attention no matter where they were from.

Many companies hired domestic scientists to demonstrate the use of their products. The Pillsbury-Washburn Co. hired some of the most talented women to promote the use of its well-known products (detail).

Official Photograohic Co., courtesy Missouri Historical Society, St. Louis.

Almost any intelligent question was rewarded with an interesting and well-articulated response. A visitor to the Corn Palace in the Missouri section of the Agriculture Building asked: "Why is that [particular] pile of corn exhibited? The grain is not large, nor even." The attending exhibitor responded confidently, "That is a variety of corn that is grown not for the grain, but for the cob. Observe the size of the cobs. They are sold to make pipes. The grain is only a byproduct."

In addition to providing answers to questions, there were actual lectures given at some of the booths. Trade journals like the *Confectioners Gazette* seemed pleased to report to their readers that: "The chocolate manufacturers attracted attention by the clever way in which their products were displayed and the young women demonstrators who gave lectures twice a day on how chocolate should be prepared. Alongside the displays of biscuits, pies, cakes, and doughnuts there will be the machinery in operation showing the manufacture of biscuits and crackers. Here, too, the domestic lecturers were employed to teach the housewives how to bake bread."

Companies that wanted to get the highest marks for credibility spent a little more money on their demonstrators and hired women who had been trained in domestic science at some of the most elite cooking schools in America. They were "informed specialists," and women listened to them with rapt attention. They were authorities, and their endorsement of a particular brand was worth every dollar invested by the companies. A Miss Burr of the Boston School of Domestic Science lectured each day on scientific cookery with chocolate at the Walter Baker Chocolate Co.'s exhibit. A graduate of the New York School of Cooking managed the Louisiana and Texas Rice Kitchen. Miss Nelly Worcester of the Boston Cooking School, along with her assistant, dressed in the bright red and white colors of the Cottolene Co. and gave lessons in the use of this lard substitute.

The Louisiana and Texas Rice Kitchen provided daily demonstrations on the use of rice. Its souvenir menu included ways to boil rice and also included rice in many different kinds of recipes.

Courtesy Max Storm.

Model Exhibits

The Exposition might have gotten a bit carried away with all its "Model" entities, but they were highly popular with visitors. Besides all those located on the Model Street, there were others that dotted the fairgrounds. In the Department of Education Building was a model kitchen installed for the service and demonstration of cooking for "defectives" — a less-than-kind-word used for people who were mentally challenged. The Indian School also had a model kitchen, where instructors demonstrated how to cook Native American foods.

No one touring all the "Models" at the Fair could afford to fly by the Model Poultry

Farm. Visitors witnessed the various processes involved in moving from an egg to the chicken on their plates. There were 330 feet of aisles showing the stages of poultry farming, not only of chickens but also of some of their feathered relatives. Processes for incubating the eggs, feeding the chickens, killing the fowl, and cooking the birds were all demonstrated at the Model Poultry Farm.

Part of what made the Model Poultry Farm so intriguing was the attached restaurant — a chicken restaurant that served poultry cooked to the specifications of the diner. Guests were invited to choose their own chickens before they (the chickens, not the guests!) went to the chopping block. The selected birds arrived on the patrons' plates exactly as ordered. If this was a bit too much realism for some of the diners, chickens could be selected from those kept in cold storage. Needless to say, the chicken restaurant was extremely popular.

On several acres at the western edge of the Fair was the Model Dairy Farm, where 100 dairy cattle roamed. At the farm, they were fed and milked as usual, but there was an educative purpose attached to these activities. Everything was measured and recorded scientifically in order to assess each cow's productivity, as well as to test several varieties of feed.

The milk was transported to the Model Creamery in the Agriculture Building, which used about 5,000 *pounds* of it per day (Liquids often were measured in pounds at the turn of the century). From behind a plate glass window, visitors watched as milk and cream were separated using the latest processes, which were a curiosity to some and a potential means of increased productivity to others. With the process from cow to cream complete, fairgoers could buy a glass of whole milk or buttermilk, ice cream, cheese, or even butter for the rolls they had picked up earlier!

The Pure Food Movement

There were no wars on terrorism or drugs in 1904. However, a war on adulterated foods had begun in the late 1800s and was reaching its zenith in 1904: The Pure Food Movement. The growing population, the increase in food packaging, and the advances in transportation expanded the grocers' markets from Main Street to all points across the nation. Because food companies were no longer regional entities, the amount of time from production to purchase was much longer than at any other time in history.

Paul Pierce, the editor of What to Eat, *was one of the symbols of the Pure Food Movement. His magazine might be likened to* Prevention *magazine today.*
Courtesy Max Storm.

Companies were doing whatever they needed to do to extend the shelf lives of their products; this created a serious division between those who manufactured food items and those who bought them. The Pure Food Movement advocated healthy food and healthy eating and crusaded against adulterants, misbranding, and fraudulent sale of foods. The motto of their flagship publication, *What to Eat*, was "Let the label tell the truth."

Pure Food advocates such as Paul Pierce, editor of *What to Eat,* made statements that would be equally popular today in many health-conscious circles: "All of us, little and big, rich and poor, need the purest and most nourishing food to fit us for the nerve-wrenching environment of modern life. Insufficient nourishment means undermined systems, weakened nerves, and impaired brain force." However, Pierce might have exaggerated the role of pure foods by proposing that the men fed on adulterated foods were responsible for the misery of the world. "A man seldom arises from a well-cooked meal and goes out and commits a crime," wrote Pierce in the April 1902 issue.

Fair organizers were not only aware of this movement, but actively promoted its concerns. Frederic Taylor, director of the agricultural and horticultural palaces, sent a memo to Pierce saying: "If there is any possible way by which this Department can be of service to the great public in the way of presenting exhibits which shall illustrate what is done in the way of adulterated foods and how adulterants may be detected, I should be more than glad to do any proper thing to make possible such an exhibit. Speaking officially for the Expo as well as for myself personally, I can say that it is the desire of the Exposition to do just such educative things as this."

Those who planned the exhibits in the Agriculture Building emphasized the value of pure foods by allocating a two-acre section to the Pure Food Exhibit. Pierce left his home and office in Minneapolis to become superintendent of these food exhibits. Many of them were managed by nonprofit groups, such as state food inspectors and members of associations like the National Association of State Dairy and Food Departments. The National Association of State Food Commissioners had a standing booth that displayed adulterated foods.

The Pure Food Exhibit displayed 50 brands of baking powders and 40 brands of catsup for the purpose of comparison. Catsup was the item that received the most criticism because many brands were made with just the skins of red and green tomatoes, starch, paste, and a chemical preservative. The exhibit exposed companies that engaged in fraudulent packaging, including bottles with indentations to reduce the amount of contents displayed on the package, and "oleomargarine" being passed off as butter.

> The Pure Food Exhibit … exposed companies that engaged in fraudulent packaging, including bottles with indentations to reduce the amount of contents displayed on the package, and "oleomargarine" being passed off as butter.

To be aligned with this movement was smart for one's health *and* business. Clean food was in. There were demonstrations for the homemaker on how to read food labels and how to cook with pure foods. There were also presentations of the scientific research being done on food processing and packaging, highlighting the detrimental effects of adulterated foods. Fairgoers who visited these displays received literature, samples, and practical take-home information.

Companies Join In

Companies that aligned themselves with the Pure Food Movement did well, and the Fair proved a good place for them to display their association with pure food. The N.K. Fairbank Co., which made Cottolene, a lard substitute from cottonseed oil, adopted a "pure food" motto: "It shortens your food, lengthens your life." Company employees gave out thousands of pieces of literature and recipe cards to fairgoers, hoping to wean them away from the animal fat they currently used. The Quaker Co. also promoted its product with an association to the movement. Unlike the familiar head shot on today's Quaker Oats container, the 1904 Quaker was a standing figure holding a sign that read, "Pure." Fairgoers could see him on products in the Quaker Co.'s booth.

The Quaker Oats logo at the beginning of the 20th century was clearly an effort to be associated with the Pure Food Movement.

Courtesy The Quaker Oats Co.

One of the most crowded booths in the Agriculture Building was the Genesee Pure Food Co. of Le Roy, N.Y., which demonstrated the many uses of its two main products, Jell-O and Jell-O Ice Cream Powder. *Cosmopolitan* declared the Jell-O booth the, "most successful and popular exhibition on the grounds." An article in *What to Eat* noted, "The first supposition might be that the popularity of the Jell-O booth is largely due to the generous plates of Jell-O and Jell-O Ice Cream so daintily served to the visitors,

Any company associated with the Pure Food Movement was sure to call attention to itself in 1904. Cottolene, a lard substitute, promised to benefit both you and your food.

Courtesy Max Storm.

but Jell-O is an education in pure food, as well as being a momentary delight to the palate of the passer-by." We know that the Jell-O of this period was flavored, but, because it won so many pure food awards, it must have been without additives.

Jell-O was also part of the burgeoning trend toward "quick food," developed to shorten the time women spent in the kitchen. "Jell-O Ice Cream Powder is a revelation to thousands of housewives who seldom have good luck making ice cream and to the thousands more who object to the expense of making ice cream in the old-fashioned way. Add a quart of milk to the powder, do a quick freeze, and you have ice cream in 10 minutes," said *What to Eat*. To those unable to see the demonstration, the Genesee Co. sent an illustrated book of recipes explaining about Jell-O and Jell-O Ice Cream Powder. "Don't give a luncheon, a dinner, a church festival, a party, a banquet," *What to Eat* urged its readers, "without having this book, as it will save one-half the expense and labor for you."

For Food Day on Sept. 28, 1904, Minnesota and South Dakota sent 5-foot-by-5-foot pieces of wool and silk dyed with the same artificial mineral coloring found in strawberry syrups, catsup, jellies, and port wines, claiming it took only about eight ounces of the coloring to die the cloth.

Government Joins In

California did its part for pure foods by sponsoring the Model Olive Oil Factory and advocating the advantages of olive oil over adulterated oils made from other mixtures. "Yes, it costs more," observed the October 1904 issue of *What to Eat*, "but it is superior in taste and health." For Food Day on Sept. 28, 1904, Minnesota and South Dakota sent 5-foot-by-5-foot pieces of wool and silk dyed with the same artificial mineral coloring found in strawberry syrups, catsup, jellies, and port wines, claiming it took only about eight ounces of the coloring to dye the cloth. Visitors could draw their own conclusions about the powerful chemicals they were unwittingly ingesting.

The most scientific contribution was the work displayed at the Bureau of Chemistry in the Government Building — the experiment of the "Poison Squad." With the help of government funding, Dr. R. Wiley of Washington, D.C., conducted tests on 12 men who volunteered their internal systems as the testing ground for various chemicals found in foods. Everything they ate or drank was weighed and recorded by the "Calculating Squad" — a group of 18 people who filled the 4,500

12-inch-by-18-inch pages on display at the Government Building. Unfortunately, the display was more extensive than the conclusions of the study. To that point, the "Poison Squad" tests had only concluded that borax, used in preserving meats and fish, was harmful to the human stomach.

Pure Food Congress

The Pure Food Congress was held from Sept. 26 to Oct. 1 in the Palace of Agriculture's hall and was sponsored by the National Association of State Dairy and Food Departments. The object of the congress was to promote uniform food standards and government controls on the manufacture and sale of foods. Legislators, food dealers, grocers, packagers, and distributors attended the congress. Their discussions had a single focus: truth in labeling.

Their passion was about to pay off. Less than two years after the lights of the Fair went out, the U.S. government enacted the Pure Food and Drug Act for the "prevention of manufacture, sale, or transportation of adulterated or misbranded or poisonous or deleterious food, drugs, medicines, and liquors."

Courtesy St. Louis Public Library.

Sarah Tyson Rorer

During most of the 184 days of the World's Fair in St. Louis, Mrs. Rorer gave cooking demonstrations to packed audiences of men and women in the basement of her East Pavilion Cafe. That Mrs. Rorer shared her tasty recipes was only half of the story, however. Her passion was for food, and she taught and wrote about every aspect of food — including articles on "Serving Dinner Without a Maid" and "Table Waiting — How to Train the Waitress." These selections show that Mrs. Rorer's audiences included women and men of privilege and as well as those who worked for them. The beginning housewife and the family matriarch with years of experience in the kitchen both came to learn from Mrs. Rorer.

Mrs. Rorer was particularly aware of the new breed of attendee to her seminars — the working woman. She prepared lectures and booklets on the use of chafing dishes and fireless cookers just for this target audience. No matter what group of

Home Helps

A
PURE FOOD
COOK BOOK

Recipes by
Mrs Mary J Lincoln   Mrs Sarah Tyson Rorer
Mrs Helen Armstrong   Lida Ames Willis
Marion Harland

PRICE 50 CENTS

people read her articles, listened to her lectures, or attended her food demonstrations, they all heard her pet theory — salads should be on every table 365 days a year. Her article in the *Philadelphia Inquirer* in January 1900 said that, "Salad greens contain salts which kept the blood in good condition. Salad is nature's lubricant; it purifies the blood and clears the complexion. People who do not eat salads have blotches, liver marks, headaches and biliousness."

"The Nation's Instructress in Dietetics and Cookery," showed that she was ahead of her time when she wrote in an 1890 issue of the *Dietetic Gazette*: "When will people learn to prevent rather than cure disease? Good muscular exercise, proper food and fresh air will do more to develop perfect forms, perfect health and perfect beauty than all the money in the world." In a 1901 issue of *Ladies' Home Journal*, she expressed her thoughts about weight control: "Improve muscular tissue through exercise. … Prevent increase in weight by cutting off starches and sugars."

Mrs. Rorer's *World's Fair Souvenir Cook Book*, like her lectures, was filled with advice as well as recipes. Some of her advice addressed the following topics:

On Meal Planning

"An appropriate and healthful bill of fare implies both taste and discrimination. A heavy soup should never be served where a large dinner is to follow. A clear, light soup should always precede a heavy dinner course. This may be preceded by raw oysters or grape fruit and followed by fish. Light entrees such as sweetbreads, croquettes, or meat patties, may follow fish, then the substantial dish, such as beef, veal, mutton, poultry, etc. with two accompanying vegetables. A service of an acid sherbert or punch now prepares the palate for a more perfect enjoyment of the game course. Blackbirds, reedbirds or any small birds may be served with the salad, but duck, woodcock, snipe or partridge should be served as a course with baked macaroni. Then the salad, a plain lettuce with French dressing, a water cracker and a small bit of old cheese. Now the desserts, puddings or ice cream, then the fruit, nuts, raisins, candy, and last the coffee, which should be very strong and served in small cups."

On Bread

"Homemade bread should consist only of flour, water or milk, yeast and salt and if properly and carefully made will be nutritious, palatable, light and very different from ordinary bakers' bread. It is necessary and very important that bread should be light and porous; to allow the juices of the stomach to have access to every part, and that digestion in all parts may be commenced at the same time. Let me tell you that yeast is a plant, and a very delicate one. Like other plants, yeast requires transplanting; you first sponge, then knead, then mould. Many are the ways of making bread … but sweetness and lightness are always the chief considerations."

On Vegetable Salads

"Any or all vegetables may be made into salads. Lettuce, sorrel, corn salad, watercress and peppergrass are best served with French dressing. Tomatoes, asparagus, string beans and potatoes are best with thick dressings."

CHAPTER 9

Supersizing at the Fair

With virtually every spot at the Fair awhirl with activity, a visitor could easily acquire a case of what might be called "Exposition Attention Deficit Disorder" — too many things to see at once. However, even the most distracted fairgoer could hardly miss Louisiana's 4-foot, 125-pound sweet potato or Missouri's 3,000-pound, 6-foot-in-diameter round of cream cheese!

There was a good reason for bringing the biggest and best of everything to the Fair and for presenting it in a big way: *People paid attention!*

This French hand-carved cask was filled with champagne.
Courtesy Yvonne Suess.

- Washington state displayed 4-foot-high celery and 4-foot-high rhubarb measuring 5 inches thick.
- Colorado exhibited strawberries that were 6 inches in circumference and potatoes that averaged 4 pounds each.
- Indiana showed four lemons weighing 7 pounds each.
- Mexico displayed 20-inch-round pineapples.
- The French brought an enormous cask of champagne holding 17,225 gallons, almost 3,500 times larger than the normal 5-gallon barrel.
- The Italians built a 40-foot high and 20-foot round wine bottle made from 1,000 quart bottles of their famous Marsalis wine, the Italian sherry that bears the name of the town in which it originated.

Texas's reputation for wanting everything supersized was well-earned, even in 1904. The state brought 12 watermelons to the Fair weighing about 1,200 pounds total. During the jury process, one watermelon could feed the 20 male jurors testing the sample. The Texas exhibit also had 47 ears of popcorn that came from nine stalks, and one stalk of ordinary corn that reached 20 feet high and was still growing while on display at the Fair.

New York had a supersized variety of foods on display. The display had 27 types of peppers, five types of cabbage, six types of eggplant, and 400 varieties of potatoes. It also displayed a 4-ton food pyramid made of the state's best pumpkins and squash.

Supersized Planning

The building that displayed most of these supersized edibles was also supersized. The Palace of Agriculture was the largest building at the Exposition, 15 percent larger than any other at the Fair. It was 1,600 feet by 400 feet, the area of 10 football fields. The height was approximately equivalent to an 8-story building. The windows alone were 75 feet tall and were 14 feet off the floor in order to accommodate large displays beneath them. The Palace of Agriculture was situated within the fairgrounds on a 70-acre site known as Agriculture Hill, along with the Palace of Horticulture and many outdoor exhibits.

The Palace of Agriculture was the largest of the 11 palaces and only one of the two to have exterior color tinting.
Official Photographic Co., courtesy Laura Brandt.

The two food palaces were also "supercolored." When it came to both the Palace of Agriculture and the Palace of Horticulture, the Exposition broke its own rule about keeping all buildings at the Fair monotone. St. Louis had already taken a step toward color by painting the exterior of the palaces ivory instead of bright white, the color used at the Columbian Exposition in Chicago. However, it went even further with the two palaces displaying food and plants. According to Frederic Taylor in David Francis's *The Universal Exposition of 1904*, "These structures are treated in color in part, and in that much differ from the other Exposition palaces, which are finished in old ivory tints." It appears that the color used for these two palaces was in the orange family, and certainly would have drawn the fair-goers' attention.

Frederic W. Taylor was director of the Palace of Agriculture and the Palace of Horticulture.

Courtesy Max Storm.

Organizing the palaces of horticulture and agriculture took a person with a supersized background in both management and the sciences. Taylor was the perfect fit for this position. He was a professor of horticulture in his native state of Nebraska and had been in charge of the Nebraska horticultural exhibit at the Chicago World's Fair.

One of most overlooked features of the Fair is one that must have taken a great deal of planning — refrigeration. The Louisiana Purchase Exposition provided the first opportunity for refrigeration to be used at an event of this magnitude. It had a phenomenal effect on how much could be displayed and how large the Fair itself could be. The majority of food exhibits displayed in the first weeks of the Fair were grown and harvested in 1903 and stored at the Fair in refrigerated units until the opening date. The *World's Fair Bulletin* reported: "Never before, at either a public or private exhibition, have there been given anything like the opportunities for so comprehensive a display ... the cold storage facilities have made it easy to do more for horticulture at this Exposition than was accomplished at the Pan-American and Columbian Expositions together."

Everything could not be preserved for the entire 7 months of the Fair, however, and states received regular shipments of replacement fruits and vegetables — via refrigerated train cars. Not everything supersized could fit into a cold storage locker either, so by the end of the summer Missouri's cream cheese, for instance, could be easily located with one's nose — making refrigeration even more appreciated!

Ways to Supersize

In addition to supersized food items, the supersizing instinct also showed up in the displays themselves. Not all the food exhibits were oversized, but often the designers used huge amounts of a particular food or used food in highly unusual ways.

Both these methods served the same purpose — they got attention. Although these displays predated The *Guinness Book of World Records*, they would have surely qualified for its pages. The creators of the "supersized" displays showed a great deal of ingenuity in creating both food forms and food sculptures.

Food Forms

Food forms were recognizable people, places, or things, created out of foodstuffs, the most frequently used being corn and corn byproducts. Builders used corn husks, corncobs, corn tassels, corn kernels, and whole corn to fashion every design imaginable. An estimated 21,000 bushels were used in displays by the corn-growing states of the Midwest.

Missouri built the Corn Palace and two corn towers. The towers, made from leaves of corn plants and corn shucks, were replicas of the Louisiana Purchase Monument, which sat at the foot of the Grand Basin. The Missouri Corn Palace, with its dome nearly 10 feet taller than the towers, was made with 1,000

This replica of the California statehouse was constructed from native crops of almonds.

Courtesy Max Storm.

Santa Clara County's exhibit included this replica of a Spanish mission made from California fruits.

Courtesy Dr. Lyndon Irwin.

bushels of differently shaded corn. It was large enough that visitors could sit inside and lounge, and it was a real crowd-drawer. It turned out to be a landmark for meeting friends or for finding lost family members.

Missouri also created life-size figures of two women with all of their clothing made from corn products. One was an Indian maiden whose outfit included a necklace made from unpopped pop-corn. The other was a lady whose corn dress was fringed with "silk."

Indiana designed a portrait of Ben-Hur and his chariot. The horses were made of corn pith, Ben-Hur of corn shucks, and the chariot of broomcorn. Even the dust raised by the racing chariot was made from corn-meal.

One California county made a mini-ature of the state capitol in prunes, and Sacramento County, known for its almonds, made a miniature of its capitol with its signature nut-meat. Santa Clara County created an old Spanish mission made of prunes, peaches, and apricots.

The most photographed and perhaps the most memorable exam-ples of supersizing with food forms were animal shapes. Visiting children would, no doubt, have found these more interesting than the corn towers. Even today, those who have only a cursory interest in the 1904 World's Fair are still taken with the "almond" elephant, the "hops" horse, and, of course, the prune bear. All of these were

This view of the nut elephant appears in Mark Bennitt's History of the Louisiana Purchase Exposition. *The caption describes the structure as the "Almond elephant."*
Courtesy Max Storm.

the creations of Californians from one county or other.

Over the years the "almond" elephant has had something of an identity crisis. Views of the life-size elephant made of California nuts appear as the "Almond Elephant" in official books, like Mark Bennitt's classic, *History of the Louisiana Purchase Exposition*, as well as in stereopticon views (the first type of viewfinder images). There are a few 1904 references, however, that call it the "Walnut Elephant." With the help of modern imaging techniques used by Bob Miano of Technisonic Studios in St. Louis and and the expertise of Dr. Shannon Smith and other horticulturists at the Missouri Botanical Gardens, efforts have been made to find out the true nature of the elephant. At this point, results are inconclusive, however, and the true identity of the elephant remains in question. An even greater identity crisis occurs with a life-size form of a horse made of "hops." Depending on which source you use, it might actually be made of pecans!

But, the prune bear? He was all prunes! The intimidating creature, standing 10 feet tall, with teeth showing and getting ready to lunge at passersby, was composed of harmless prunes. He attracted

This view of the elephant appeared on the popular stereopticon views sold as souvenir items. The caption on the stereo calls the elephant the "Walnut elephant" (above).

This life-size food form of a horse is sometimes described as the horse made of hops, and, other times, from pecans (left).
Courtesy Yvonne Suess.

The infamous prune bear with three of California's commissioners in charge of the state's exhibits in the Palace of Horticulture.

Jessie Tarbox Beals, courtesy Missouri Historical Society, St. Louis.

visitors to demonstrations of cooking prunes as well as to the free literature on the benefits and uses of the dried fruit.

Food Sculptures

If food could be used to form images, why not sculpt it? Designers began with large blocks of food and sculpted them into murals, busts, dioramas, bas-reliefs, and life-size images of historical people. The most popular medium was butter.

Butter sculpting was not new to the 1904 Fair. Visitors to both Chicago and Buffalo, as well as to all the dairy expositions, had seen plenty of butter sculpting. What they had not seen before was the new process of preserving the masterpieces. Previously, the sculptures were kept in cases cooled by blocks of ice, but the St. Louis Fair was the first to use mechanical refrigeration for this purpose. Visitors watched sculptors work in cooled areas or viewed finished products that had been sculpted elsewhere and brought to the refrigerated cases. Triple plate glass separated the viewer from the butter images.

Most of the sculptures were formed with butter (All 10 tons of it!) slathered over forms made of wood, wire, and cheesecloth. Some of the sculptors were popular in their native states, and others were nationally known artists of the time. C.F. Froliche, who studied in Paris and had his studio in New York, did the famous butter bust of Roosevelt. Illinois sponsored the dual busts of President Lincoln and President Grant with the Liberty Bell. And Minnesota contributed Father Hennepin and an Indian in a canoe discovering the falls of St. Anthony.

North Dakota provided the famous life-size butter sculpture of Roosevelt on horseback as a Rough Rider in the Spanish-American War.

Butter was not the only medium. Louisianans sculpted "Miss Louisiana" from a giant sugar cube. An unidentified newspaper article from Taylor's fourth scrapbook describes Miss Louisiana: "She is a sweet lass. She stands nearly five feet tall, just the accepted size for the model female figure and is the product of a sculptor who knows the proper proportions." Miss Louisiana perhaps could not take the pressure of being so perfect because, by August, she began to fall apart. The summer heat made her ear drop off, and the commissioners could not figure

This milkmaid with her cow was one of many butter sculptures in the dairy section of the Palace of Agriculture. An observer was looking through triple plate glass into the huge refrigerator storing the dairy displays.

Courtesy Yvonne Suess.

a way to stop the process. It looked as if she would end up in fairgoers' iced tea before the end of the Exposition!

In July, the *Republic* reported that "Miss Utah" was also fighting for her life. However, it was her weight that was the issue. Miss Utah was sculpted from beeswax, and the summer heat caused her to get soft, pliant, and lose her Miss Utah figure. Refrigeration was the answer for her, and she did make it to cold storage. But she carried quite a bit of baggage with her — the state coat of arms, a beehive, the American eagle, the American flag, and several emblems of the bee industry — all done in beeswax.

Lot's wife (a figure from the Bible) fared better at the Fair than she did in biblical history. She was carved from a solid block of rock salt from Louisiana. She glittered in the lights, but appeared scared as she turned and looked backwards, doing exactly what she had been told not to do! Lot's wife weighed about 850 pounds, and her pedestal weighed 400 pounds. She was able to keep herself together at the Palace of Mines and Metallurgy for the duration of the Fair.

> "Sanguine persons hoped that we had outgrown this sort of grotesque childishness and were learning that the proper place for beans and butter and the like farm products is not in the sculptor's studio."

Supersized Criticism

Not everyone was enamored with using food to build and sculpt. An unknown writer for the *New York Daily News* had some acerbic remarks to make about the whole enterprise: "Nearly 20 [actually 11] years ago at Chicago, sundry statues made of ears of corn, cans of vegetables, tablets of beef extract and such unholy materials were 'features of the Exposition.' Now it is proposed by a California town to send an elk made of beans to the St. Louis show. Sanguine persons hoped that we had outgrown this sort of grotesque childishness and were learning that the proper place for beans and butter and the like farm products is not in the sculptor's studio. If the talent applied to this sort of nonsense were employed in work on proper material, one of two things would be accomplished. Either the artist would find that he was not so much of an artist after all, or other people would discover that he really had talent and might assist him to make something of it."

Reasons for Supersizing

Supersizing displays of foods or displaying foods that had been supersized was done to get visitor attention for reasons that fell into two main categories: economics and immigration, and pride and competition. There was a less-striking reason, too. Some states wanted to strut their displays in hopes that they would be picked for a future convention site or even a world's fair site.

Economics and Immigration

Many of the states and territories wanted more people — especially farmers. Agriculture could make a state rich. Oklahoma, not yet qualified for statehood, had a sign on its exhibit that said, "Wanted, more farmers to grow Oklahoma products."

The California counties, too, were hungry for more fruit growers, livestock ranchers, and farmers. In *History of the Louisiana Purchase Exposition*, Bennitt wrote, "The object of the display was to induce immigration, as the flexibility of the county [of Sacramento] will support at least 10 times the population, and the county is bound to become one of the greatest dairying and fruit districts of the world."

Besides Missouri, California occupied more exhibit space than any other state or company in the Agriculture Building. Californians were aggressive marketers for increased population to their state. There was even competition among the counties of California for the attention of the visitors: "The Los Angeles County Chamber of Commerce had a booth completely

Los Angeles County constructed this booth from the county's bounty of fruits, vegetables, seeds, and nuts. The booth used dark green velvet as a backdrop for the bright-colored oranges and lemons that bordered the exhibit. The fruits were continually replaced with fresh specimens.

Courtesy Max Storm.

covered in dark green velvet," Bennitt wrote. "The 20-foot wings on the booth and the 45-foot towers were covered with this dark green velvet like the foliage of an orange tree. Outlining its dome was a border of fresh oranges; a portico of peanuts stretched from pillar to pillar and between these from gold branches hung glass jars filled with yellow honey."

Some states went to great lengths to attract attention to themselves. The commissioner from Washington state was determined to present the *best* quality fruits. A grower had reported to him that he had 85 mammoth cherries weighing 4 pounds apiece. To assure that there would be no time lost in transferring the fruit from tree to jar, the commissioner personally drove his wagon through the orchards, carrying all the necessary equipment to preserve the fruit. Nine oversized jars, each containing approximately 35 pounds of the cherries, were put up right there on the grower's grounds and then sent to St. Louis for display.

For Oklahoma Day, Mr. C.A. McNabb, who was in charge of the Oklahoma display in the Agriculture Building, wrote to the secretary of the territory of Oklahoma in 1903 with a request: "Please plan to send watermelons between 50-100 or more pounds!" He wanted 100 of them. McNabb wanted to put Oklahoma on the map, literally, as a state, and he was determined that Sept. 6, Oklahoma Day, would be a memorable occasion. The watermelons would be cut up in slices and given to visitors at the Oklahoma Building on the fairgrounds. McNabb even told them how to get the watermelons that big: "Pinch off all the buds except a couple from the vine. Give the roots lots of water."

> Juliana's main purpose in coming to St. Louis was to secure California as the next site for the influential National Butter Makers' Convention.

Californians provided the Fair with an experience that could definitely be classified as a supersized, one-of-a-kind event concerning food — well, almost food. It involved their delegate to the National Butter Makers Convention, met by hundreds of people at the train station. Some were generally curious and some wanted a good look at her body. She arrived in a private car and left the train with her lifelong companion, Charles D. Pierce. Juliana de Kol headed for her private suite, where she would stay for the remainder of the Fair. Her reputation preceded this convention delegate. She was the kind no one could miss in a crowd. Miss Juliana de Kol was a cow — a Holstein-Friesian cow — that had broken all records for producing the most milk in a series of tests. Juliana's main purpose in coming to St. Louis was to secure California as the next site for the influential National Butter Makers Convention.

Competition and Pride

Many exhibitors had proven themselves as "best in class" before they were selected to come to the Fair. Many of these competitors brought their prize food products to the "Big Fair." Awards at the Exposition's juried events were highly valued and sought out by both small producers and large companies. Anyone receiving a medal (and thousands were awarded) went back and "showed the folks at home." Companies used these recognitions on their promotional materials to impress customers in a highly competitive national market.

Other competitions were on a smaller scale. The West Plains Missouri Commercial Club won "best in its class" in a local competition and was chosen as the delegation to accompany a railroad car of peaches for Peach Day at the Fair. The Iowa Corn Club — four neighboring farmers — sent its prize six ears of corn to the Fair to see how they compared with corn from neighboring states.

It might have been easy for visitors to lose a discriminating eye when faced with row upon row of corn displays, but it was hardly possible for one display from Illinois to go unnoticed. In 1903, the League of Corn Growers challenged young boys to a contest to see who could produce the most exceptional ears of corn. The league sent them seeds, and the boys recorded their methods of planting, their experiences during the growing and harvesting season, and their conclusions.

Eight thousand boys took the challenge, and 1,700 entered their 1903 crop for competition. The superintendent of the Illinois exhibit brought the corn for display, but added a feature that touched even the weariest fairgoer's heart. Photographs of the young corn growers accompanied many of their crops on display and personalized their efforts.

Members of the Jury for India Teas.
Courtesy Max Storm.

The Towles Log Cabin Syrup Co. offered cash prizes and recipe booklets to visitors guessing the number of the company maple syrup cans in its exhibit cabin.

Courtesy Max Storm.

Jury Process

Thousands of entries in every category displayed at the Fair were judged by men and women selected as jurors. Much like today, jurors visited, tasted, smelled, and observed every entry. There were standards or criteria for every class of entry, whether it was bread, dairy, chicken, fruit, tea, coffee, or wine. Those who entered their prized products took the competition seriously, and they expected the jurors to do the same.

The Contests

The contests at the Fair were just for fun, of course. Mary Franke of St. Louis correctly guessed the Opening Day attendance (187,793) and won a gold watch her descendants still treasure. Four thousand people tried to guess the number of beans in the California shield at the state's exhibit. First prize was a case of olive oil; second was a sack of beans.

The Towles Log Cabin Syrup Co. had another counting contest and distributed $600 and recipe books as prizes to Exposition visitors who came nearest to estimating the number of cans of syrup filling its log cabin exhibit.

The Mellin's Food Co. had a delightfully different kind of contest. Beside its products were 20 baby pic-

The Mellin's Food Co.'s popular contest had visitors guessing the gender of the children in baby pictures displayed at its booth.

Courtesy Dr. Lyndon Irwin.

tures. The contest was to guess which ones were boys and which ones were girls. The prize was $250.

A *Los Angeles Herald* reporter observed, "There are two very handsome French oil paintings in the Paris Salon and wonderful statuary [in the Palace of Fine Arts], but the guessing contest is the more popular attraction." Some things never change!

And the bear raises his pruney head again! The game here, as you would suspect, was to guess the number of prunes covering the bear's plaster frame. A circular with a picture of the prune bear and information about Sacramento Valley was given to each guest who signed the register at the booth. The name, address, and guess were recorded. Guesses ranged from 6,000 to 1 million prunes. On Nov. 3, 1904, the *Globe-Democrat* reported the results of the prune bear contest: "The first place winner was from Virginia and guessed the exact number of prunes, 14,265 prunes. F.W. Castle of St. Louis guessed the second closest, 14,263." The *Globe-Democrat* did not record the prize, but given the reverence for this fruit, an educated guess might be — prunes!

One contest entrant guessed the exact number of prunes in the "prune bear contest."
Courtesy Yvonne Suess.

Supersized Heart

After all the efforts to get the attention of the public and jurors with supersizing the bounty of the earth, it would be easy to lose sight of the little things. Colvin Brown, the exhibit director who brought Juliana de Kol to the Fair, received a letter from Myrtle Crozier of St. Louis. The *Sparta (Ill.) Argonaut* printed the request: "Dear Sir: I see by the papers that you are in charge of the San Joaquin County exhibit, and I write to ask you if we can get married in your booth. My fiance is coming from New Orleans next Wednesday and we will be married at once. I was born in San Joaquin County near Stockton, and I think it would be fine to be married there in your booth, as it would be just like home. I know my sweetheart will agree with me. Yours truly, Myrtle T. Crozier." The *Argonaut* reported that, "Mr. Brown is quite willing to accommodate the couple, and says that he will buy the license and pay the minister for performing the ceremony and that he will furnish a band to play, 'In the Valley of San Joaquin' in lieu of the wedding march."

Sarah Tyson Rorer

None of the literature records that Mrs. Rorer was ever involved in supersizing foods in any way. But over the years she herself became supersized, as it were, due to the ever-growing sphere of her influence. Mrs. Rorer literally went from basement to "big top." In the early days, many of her lectures were done in lower-level kitchens, but, as she drew larger and larger crowds, she needed larger and larger venues. In the biography, *Sarah Tyson Rorer: The Nation's Instructress in Dietetics and Cookery*, Emma Seifrit Weigley wrote: "As the fame of Sarah Tyson Rorer and her demonstrations spread, she was called upon to appear throughout the US. In 1891 she gave two series of seventeen lectures each at the Lenox Lyceum. The next year she presented a course of lectures at the Johnson Building on Flatbush Avenue in Brooklyn. In the fall of 1895 she attracted throngs to the Concert Hall of Madison Square Garden. In the spring of 1896 and again in 1897 she shuttled between the Lyric Hall and the Harlem Opera House."

"As the fame of Sarah Tyson Rorer and her demonstrations spread, she was called upon to appear throughout the US."

Her influence was extended even more when she began delivering weekly radio shows on home economics and cooking techniques in the 1920s. By 1924, she was so well known that a Broadway musical, *Sitting Pretty* by Jerome Kern and lyricist P.G. Wodehouse, included a song called "Mr. and Mrs. Rorer." The verses included the following:

"When Mister Rorer came home feeling mad
Kind Missis Rorer was not scared or sad
With love light beaming in her eyes
She spoke to him of Pumpkin pies
And then went off and planked a wicked shad!

When Mister Rorer said that he was blue
Kind Missis Rorer filled him up with stew
And there'd be no divorce today
If only wives would act the way
That kind Missis Rorer used to do."

Weigley went on to note that Sarah Tyson Rorer was the guest of honor at the 1925 Woman's World's Fair held in Chicago. There, on "Cook's Day," all the exhibitors and demonstrators in the domestic science booths gave special honor to Mrs. Rorer. She was 75 at the time and still managed to give a lecture that day on radio station WMAQ in Chicago.

Although she did not supersize food herself, she certainly would have known what to do with the supersized food at the Fair. Here are some recipes from her *World's Fair Souvenir Cook Book*:

Salted Almonds

"After they are blanched, spread them over the bottom of a baking-pan, add the smallest amount of butter to lightly grease them, put them in a very moderate oven, and bake slowly until thoroughly dried and a golden brown, take them from the fire, dust them thickly with fine salt, turn them on a cool dish, and stand in a cold place."

Sweet Potato Croquettes

"Boil four good-sized sweet potatoes. When done, peel and mash them through a colander, add one tablespoonful of butter, one teaspoon of salt, a dash of cayenne, and four tablespoonfuls of cream. Beat until light, form into croquettes. Dip first into beaten egg and then in breadcrumbs, and fry in smoking hot fat."

Stewed Peaches (All Kinds of Dried Fruit May be Cooked in the Same Manner)

"If the peaches are clean do not wash them, but if they look dusty wash quickly in cold water, then cover with fresh cold water, soak overnight, and cook in the same water until they are tender. Sweeten to taste."

Celery Soup

"Wash six or eight green stalks of celery and cut them into small pieces, using the leaves as well, cover with a pint of boiling water and boil thirty minutes; then press through a colander, do not drain; but allow the water to go through with the celery. Put one quart of milk in a double boiler, add the celery and water and a tablespoonful of onion juice; rub one large tablespoonful of butter and three even tablespoonfuls of flour to a smooth paste, add a little of the soup until a liquid is formed, then turn into the double boiler, stir continually until it thickens, add salt and pepper to taste, and serve immediately. This is delicious if properly made."

CHAPTER 10

Truths, Half-Truths, and Anything but the Truth

The approaching centennial of the 1904 World's Fair has caused another wave of theories about "food firsts" — those foods that were supposedly introduced at the Fair. More and more "legends" are appearing in print and are being spread at an even more rapid pace via the World Wide Web. To the already popular list of "first foods" — the ice cream cone, iced tea, the hot dog, the hamburger, Dr Pepper, and peanut butter — we are now told to add the club sandwich, Heinz pickles, and, believe it or not, sliced bread!

... but the question remains for the curious reader and the Fair buff alike: "What foods really were introduced at the Fair?"

Food, as we've seen, gave a stellar performance at the Fair. It was a source of enjoyment, camaraderie, pride, and adventure. It provided sustenance to those who walked or worked the fairgrounds and offered buyer and manufacturer an uncommon opportunity to meet face to face. That is no small contribution to the history of food, but the question remains for the curious reader and the Fair buff alike: "What foods really were introduced at the Fair?"

This may seem like a simple question, but food history is amazingly complex because it is not always easy to determine when, where, or in what form various foods made their appearance on menu or table. Having to concede that "invented" and "birthplace of" were not really accurate words to describe some of the "food firsts" associated with the Fair, "popularized" has become the new word of choice. But, to say that all the foods in question were just "popularized" is to err in the other direction. Credit should be given where credit is due. Some of the "food firsts" actually were firsts, some were "sort of" firsts, some *were* "popularized," and others were commonplace long before 1904.

Definitely Not the First

In 1949, the *Post-Dispatch* announced the 45th anniversary of the invention of **iced tea** in St. Louis. When the Tea Bureau, Inc., in New York held its 1951 competition for "Miss Iced Tea," only St. Louis women could enter the race. The Tea Bureau was affirming the theory that the Fair was, indeed, the birthplace of iced tea.

Here's how the story, as it is recorded in a number of sources, unfolds: Richard Blechynden, the special commissioner from the India Tea Association, was in the business of selling the traditional hot drink. During the hot summer of 1904, his hot tea was not exactly in demand. So he seized the moment by sending his Singhalese waiters out with tea and ice cubes in glasses — offering a refreshing new drink. Hence, the beginning of "iced" tea!

Visitors enter the highly popular East India Pavilion, where tea was served or purchased in bulk. Richard Blechynden was the commissioner from India in charge of this pavilion, and the sale of tea was done by the India Tea Association.

Courtesy Laura Brandt.

Even the most liberal World's Fair buff acknowledges that this story and the accolade "new" attributed to the drink might be a bit exaggerated. Many suggest that Blechynden did not invent the drink, but "popularized" it, or, as some say now, "re-invented" it. ("Re-invented" is a curious term that begs the question: Can something be re-invented once it has been invented?)

The India Tea Association sold loose tea in these containers with the directions on how to prepare tea printed on the outside of the can.

Shara (Jessie) Storm, courtesy Max Storm.

Some facts about iced tea:

1. Both hot tea and iced tea appeared on most menus at the Fair — at the Barbecue, Fair Japan, the Old Irish Parliament House, the Louisiana and Texas Rice Kitchen, Mrs. Rorer's East Pavilion Cafe, and so on. It is highly unlikely that all these restaurants jumped on the bandwagon of Blechynden's "new idea," and scurried to the print shops to have their menus reprinted!

2. Blechynden was hardly a desperate tea vendor! In fact, he was the highest-ranking representative from India and the director of the East India Pavilion.

He also had a concession selling East India Tea in liquid and loose form. His waiters were not Singhalese (from Ceylon), but were turbaned and bearded natives of India who were clad in white and who served their customers in balcony cafes rather than on the streets.

3. In 1901, when the Exposition planners visited the Buffalo Pan-American Exposition, the Pullman Dining Car Service listed iced tea on its menu. This was not an obscure railroad service, and it can be assumed that its many diners were familiar with the beverage.

4. At the two previous fairs in Buffalo in 1901 and in Chicago in 1893, the Enterprising Manufacturing Co. of Pennsylvania distributed thousands of its popular recipe booklet, *The Enterprising Housekeeper*. In the booklet, the company advertised its popular ice shredder's many uses — one of which was "for your iced tea."

The iced tea recipe from this souvenir cookbook of the Chicago Columbian Exposition in 1893 suggests using "English Breakfast" or "Best Japanese" teas to make the "best of this drink."

Author's collection.

5. Concessionaire No. 293 in Chicago — an N.B. Reed — had a concession that grossed over $2,000. His wares? Iced tea and lemonade.

6. The *Home Queen World's Fair Souvenir Cook Book* from the Chicago World's Fair includes a recipe for variations on serving iced tea. Other cookbooks dating back to the 1880s do the same. Some food historians claim that iced teas appeared in Southern cuisine even earlier than that.

7. Dr. Lyndon Irwin, from Southwest Missouri State University, posts an article on his website from the *Nevada (Mo.) Noticer* (1890) that lists 880 gallons of iced tea served at a reunion of Confederate soldiers.

The Pullman Dining Car Service listed iced tea on its bill of fare in 1901.

Courtesy Max Storm.

Louisiana Purchase Exposition Co.

Dedicatory Excursion

To Pan - American Exposition

.. July 2, 1901 ..

Leave St. Louis . 2.30 p m, June 30th   Leave Buffalo . . 2.30 p m, July 4th
Arrive Buffalo . . 8.00 a m, July 1st   Arrive St. Louis . 8.00 a m, July 5th

·· VIA ··

C. C. C. & St. L. and Lake Shore Roads.

Pullman Dining Car Service

D I N N E R

Mock Turtle	Consomme, Clear
Cucumbers	Young Onions

Baked Lake Trout, Fine Herbs

Potatoes Parisienne

Soft Shell Crabs on Toast   Baked Spaghetti, Italienne

Prime Roast Beef, Au Jus

Roast Duckling

Boiled Potatoes	Braised Sweet Potatoes
Green Corn	Buttered Beets

Lobster Salad, au Mayonnaise

Chilled Water Melon

Neapolitan Ice Cream	Assorted Cake
Marmalade	English Wafers
Canadian and Edam Cheese	Bent's Water Crackers

Coffee   Tea   Iced Tea

En Route, June 30, 1901.

What really "stirs the pot" is that a "Richard Blechynden" was listed as an official concession-aire (No. 325) "to serve tea in cups and packages" at the Chicago World's Fair in 1893 — 11 years before the one in St. Louis. The financial records from the exposition do not list any ledger entries for Blechynden — which raises the question of whether he actually showed up or was just late with his report. But, if he had been there, it would have been odd that he would not have realized that his product was already being sold in hot and cold versions. It would likewise be odd that, in the 11 intervening years, he would have been totally oblivious to the drink's inclusion in cookbooks and on menus.

Duane Sneddeker, director of library and archives for the Missouri Historical Society in St. Louis and co-author of *From the Palaces to the Pike*, believes, "It was during the post-WW II years, that St. Louisans were look-ing nostalgically at the 'good old days' and began lionizing some of the stories told about the Fair." This same time period came upon the heels of the popular 1944 movie, *Meet Me in St. Louis*, which so prominently featured the 1904 World's Fair. The story of "iced tea" was a good addition to its lore. There is the very real possibility, however, that Blechynden would be the first to say, "What was I supposed to have done?" and that the real inventor will never be known.

The Enterprise Ice Shredder

For Shaving Ice Coarse or Fine

No. 33, Tinned	.	50 cents
No. 34, Nickel-Plated,	.	$1.25

Our Ice Shredder is operated by simply drawing the blade over a piece of ice, the pressure applied producing fine or coarse pieces, as desired. No necessity for taking the ice out of the refrigerator, as the cup can be filled from the side, end or top of a cake of ice without disturbing anything or wetting the hands. Its use will be appreciated for Fruits, Drinks, Oysters and Clams on half-shell, Olives, Celery, Radishes, Iced Tea, Sliced Tomatoes, etc., and many purposes in the sick-room.

The Enterprising Manufacturing Co. gave thousands of these recipe booklets to visitors at the 1901 Pan-American Exposition in Buffalo. The ad in the booklet suggested that the company's ice shred-der would be useful in the preparation of iced tea.

Courtesy Fred Lavin.

What about the **hot dog**? It turns out to have a history that is pretty much like iced tea's, only a lot less straight-forward. It is important to note that, at the turn of the century, a hot dog was a sausage on a bun, and that combination was actually referred to as a "hot dog." The little reddish ones we know today did not come along until much later, but they and their sausage predecessors definitely shared the same name.

> 1893 was a big year for the hot dog, well in advance of the St. Louis Fair.

Here's how the story associating the birth of the hot dog with the 1904 Fair is often told: Concessionaire Anton Feuchtwanger (he really was there) ran out of the white gloves he had been giving to patrons so they would not burn their fingers on the hot meat. Because so many people walked off with the gloves, he asked his brother-in-law, a baker, to create a holder — a bun — for the hot dog. And from then on the two were a marriage made on earth!

Some facts about the hot dog:

1. Feuchtwanger, — the Anton from the story above — actually did improvise a bun for the frankfurter in St. Louis — but it was in 1883!
2. Hot dog historian (Yes, there is one!) Bruce Kraig, Ph.D., names the college magazines of the late 1800s as the place where the term "hot dog" began appearing in print. At Yale in the fall of 1894, references were made to the then-accepted practice of "dog wagons" selling "hot dogs."
3. There is more than enough evidence to show that the hot dog was served on a bun in New York by Charles Feltman at Coney Island in the late 1800s. The Coney Island Hot Dog was apparently not just a local delicacy because it was sold at the East Indian Congress Restaurant at the Pan-American Fair in 1901.
4. 1893 was a big year for the hot dog, well in advance of the St. Louis Fair. It was the year of the Columbian Exposition, and people consumed large quantities of sausage sold by vendors because it was both convenient and inexpensive. In that year, also, the hot dog became popular at baseball parks. The connection was made by Chris Von de Ahe, a German immigrant, who owned a St. Louis bar as well as the St. Louis Browns Major League baseball team.
5. The minutes of the Exposition show that multiple vendors received the rights to

sell their "sausage and frankfurter sandwiches," including a company called the Armour Packing Co., located in East St. Louis, Ill.

6. Kraig credits the German immigrants for the fare as well as the name. They brought not only their sausages but their dachshund dogs to America. The Germans themselves called the frankfurter a "little dog" and began the association with their meat. Kraig is one of many researchers who completely reject most theories about the genesis of the hot dog, including the St. Louis story.

So it would have been very hard for the St. Louis World's Fair to be the birthplace of what was already in existence and what already had a very public presence. It makes a great story, but it is just not accurate.

Other less well-known myths about the name "hot dog" can hopefully be dispelled forever as well. One is the association with an item of the Igorots' diet. There is no possible basis for such a literal interpretation of the term "hot dog." Another fallacious story grew up around the nickname for a section of St. Louis located near the fairgrounds called "Dogtown." For years there was a legend that this was a popular source of dinner meat for the Igorots. However, according to Virginia Lopez, secretary of the Dogtown Historical Society, and Bob Corbett, Dogtown historian and professor emeritus of philosophy, the name came from the large number of hounds that acted as guard dogs for families of working men who were away at their jobs. Because Dogtown was near a railway, transients made their way through the town looking for handouts, and the dogs were protection from them. But there is no record of the Igorots being there at all. In a largely Caucasian section of town, the small-framed, dark-complected Igorots would definitely have been noticed.

> The Germans themselves called the frankfurter a "little dog" and began the association with their meat.

"Popularized" in Varying Degrees

We've already seen that the Fair was a marketing director's dream come true. So it makes sense that some foods did actually grow in popularity because of their exposure at the Fair. But not all of them became popular to the same extent. Here are some of their stories:

Dr Pepper became popular during and after the Fair due not to some stroke of

While at the World's Fair

DRINK

"Dr. Pepper"

KING OF BEVERAGES

❡ We are establishing agencies throughout the entire country to bottle this celebrated beverage for us. ❡ If interested in the bottling of carbonated drinks, call on us while in St. Louis. Our office number is

816 North Sixteenth Street, St. Louis, Mo., U.S.A.

Telephone
Kinloch
B 775

This ad for "Dr. Pepper" appeared in many issues of the World's Fair Bulletin. The period after "Dr" was dropped when the company redesigned its logo in 1950.

Author's collection.

luck, but due to an entirely premeditated plan. The formula for the carbonated soda had been the result of a pharmacist "playing" with fruit flavorings for soda water much as children today might mix different soft drinks to come up with a "new soda." Charles Alderton was that pharmacist and he worked with Wade Morrison in a Waco, Texas, drugstore. The two pharmacists joined forces and sold the concoction to the townspeople of Waco. When they found they could not keep it in stock, it was time to seek a bottler, get a patent, and form a company to sell their "Dr. Pepper." With bottler Robert Lazenby, Morrison formed the Artesian Manufacturing and Bottling Co. in 1891, and within 10 years, set up

The Liquid Carbonic Co.'s soda fountain was a popular rest spot for tired fair-goers. Carbonated sodas including Hires root beer, Coca-Cola, and Dr Pepper were sold at these soda fountains.

Official World's Fair Photographic Co., courtesy Missouri Historical Society, St. Louis.

another bottling plant in St. Louis. Already in 1901, ads for Dr Pepper appeared in the *World's Fair Bulletin*, which was being published to document the construction of the Fair. The company received a concession to sell Dr Pepper at both soda fountains and booths, and so the 13-year-old soft drink made its world premier on the St. Louis stage.

There is no definite story on the Dr Pepper name. However, we do know that Dr. Charles Pepper was Mr. Morrison's first employer in Rural Retreat, Va., when he was newly graduated from pharmacy school. Whatever the source of the name, there was a definite plan to bring the Waco- and St. Louis-based carbonated soda to the marketplace at the Fair, and, from all appearances, the risk paid off for the two men. They had, indeed, popularized their product.

What about **peanut butter**? One of the last concessionaires to get a lease from the Exposition was No. 587, C.H. Sumner, and no records show that he had any competitors for his product. Peanut butter apparently had come back full circle to St. Louis within the 14-year period between 1890 and 1904. In 1890, a St. Louis physician (name unknown) encouraged George Bayle, a food manufacturer, to make nut butter for people who needed a good source of protein but couldn't chew. He sold it for 6 cents a pound. Between 1894 and 1896, the Kellogg Co. of Battle Creek, Mich., published recipes and information on using the nut butter, but sold the product without much success.

> Peanut butter apparently had come back full circle to St. Louis within the 14-year period between 1890 and 1904.

An employee of Kellogg seized the moment and developed better grinding and processing methods, forming the Lambert Food Co., which marketed the improved product. During the same time period, Dr. George Washington Carver developed several hundred uses for peanuts, one of which could have been as a butter. So was it Sumner's small concession booth that made peanut butter popular? Or might it have been the confluence of his endeavor, the Lambert Food Co.'s sales, and Dr. Carver's work? We do know Sumner made $705 minus the $200 he owed the Exposition. That is over $10,000 in today's money; so his product was at least somewhat popular at the Fair. But it would be hard to credit the Fair alone with the invention or popularization of peanut butter.

How about the **hamburger**? Most food historians will dismiss any one city, cafe, or event as the place where hamburgers were invented or made popular, but four cities claim birthing rights to the hamburger: St. Louis, Athens, Texas, New Haven, Conn., and Seymour, Wis. Because whole books have been written on the genesis of the burger, we will focus here only on the St. Louis story, which, as you will see, is linked to the Athens, Texas, story.

The St. Louis story is the one researched and told by the late Texas historian Frank X. Tolbert in his book, *Tolbert's Texas*. In the chapter, "The Henderson County Hamburger," he tells of an Athens man by the name of Fletcher Davis, aka "Old Dave," who shaped ground meat into a patty, fried it, and served it between two slices of a bread product at his lunch counter. The story goes that he had a concession on the Pike selling his sandwich. A *New York Tribune* reporter wrote from the Fair about a new sandwich called a "hamburger" and referred to it as, "the innovation of a food vendor on the Pike." The vendor's name was not given in the article, but Tolbert reported seeing a picture from a resident of Athens whose grandfather had been to the Fair. In the grandfather's writing was "Old Dave's Hamburger Stand." Therefore, the theory was that the hamburger sandwich was "invented" in Athens, and was made popular (and even was named "hamburger") at the St. Louis World's Fair.

> It is conceivable that the Fair helped make the hamburger patty more popular by exposing a locally popular sandwich known in a number of places to millions of people.

Mrs. Rorer's illustration for preparing meat to use in her recipe for "Hamburg steak." Illustration from Mrs. Rorer's New Cook Book, 1902. Author's collection.

The story goes on. The naming was done by the St. Louis Germans, who were from Southern Germany. They looked down on Northern Germans (Fletcher Davis's heritage) and used the derogatory term associated with the Northern German city of Hamburg, i.e., "raw meat eaters." (It is true that in the old country they had learned to eat raw beef from the Tartars — as in "steak Tartar.") The St. Louis Germans then dubbed Old Dave's sandwich the "hamburger," and apparently it stuck.

Some facts about the hamburger:

1. By current definition, the hamburger is a formed piece of ground meat between a bun. Old Dave served his hamburger steak between two pieces of toast!

2. We know Old Dave shaped the meat into patties because there is evidence he did this at his lunch counter back home, but he did not invent ground beef or even "Hamburg steak." *Mrs. Rorer's New Cook Book*, a 1902 classic and a kitchen staple at that time, included not only a recipe for "Hamburg Steak," but also illustrations of the cut of meat to be used and the meat grinder with which to grind it.

3. There is no Fletcher Davis on the official concessionaire's list or on the final financial balance sheet of the LPE Co., and the company certainly would not have let anyone exert any kind of "squatter's rights."

4. Nevertheless, the McDonald's Corp. credits an unknown vendor on the Pike in 1904 as initiating its signature product.

Could anyone else in the country have thought of pressing ground beef into a patty? Yes, and we know that someone did. Could anyone else in the country have thought to put it on a bun? More than likely, but we don't know who. Could anyone else have called it a "hamburger"? This may be have been a genuine innovation at the time of the Fair, although we do not exactly know how it came about. Whoever combined burger and bun and christened it "hamburger" had millions of people stopping by and taking the idea home. It is conceivable that the Fair helped make the hamburger patty more popular by exposing a locally popular sandwich known in a number of places to millions of people.

Although the history of the **club sandwich** is not as complex as the hamburger, it, too, has been associated with the St. Louis World's Fair. In fact, popular tales credit the owners of the Tyrolean Alps Restaurant with its invention. But we can say with certainty that it did not get its start there. The most reliable food historians give credit to the Saratoga Country Club, Saratoga Springs, N.Y., for first serving the double-decker delight about 10 years before the Fair. It is unlikely that the Tyrolean Alps even had its own version, because it was never listed under "sandwiches" on the restaurant's menu. An additional twist in the story comes from finding that other

restaurants did have club sandwiches on their menus. Mrs. McCready's Model Restaurant, the American Inn, included in its sandwich fare "The American Inn Club." The Old Parliament House had a "Special Club Sandwich," and even Fair Japan had "The Club Sandwich." So the Fair may have done its part in popularizing this sandwich not through one specific concessionaire, but through many.

At the far end of the popularization spectrum is a product that did not need the Fair's help. In fact, Henry J. Heinz would take umbrage over the idea that his **pickle** was popularized at the Fair. Heinz started his company in 1870 with full intention of putting the company's products in front of the consumer in every grocery store in America. In a 1999 article by Harvard Business School professor, Nancy Koehn, the H.J. Heinz Co., is heralded as the first company in the U.S. to use highly successful brand-recognition strategies before the advent of technology. H.J. Heinz's pickles were packed with plenty of popularity before 1904.

Heinz advertising piece given to visitors to the Heinz exhibit in the Palace of Agriculture.

Author's collection.

And lastly, **sliced bread**. Bread had been being sliced with one or other implement for probably about 10,000 years. The electric slicing machine wasn't invented until 1910; so the Fair could hardly be associated with either the practice or the mechanical means of slicing bread.

The "Sort-of" Firsts

Although there were some new foods introduced at the Fair, they can only be considered "sort of firsts" because they did not receive a lot of "flashy" press over the years or eventually make it to "national icon" status. In fact, some of them even bombed!

The *Cleveland Leader* announced to its readers, "The Californians introduced a new fruit called the **kumquat** — a cross between a lemon and an orange." The Californians displayed live trees with the fruit in their exhibit in the Agriculture Building. The fruit, resembling a miniature orange, never reached great heights of popularity after the Fair. But during the Fair kumquats were extremely popular with souvenir hunters, who found them ripe to pick and pocket because of their small size. After replacing the once-filled kumquat trees three times, the Californians gave up and closed the booth.

The *Paducah (Ken.) Times* recorded that a fairly new, but rarely seen fruit was being displayed in Florida's small exhibit in the Agriculture Building: the **grapefruit** (then called the "pommel"). The fruit was not sold in the North until a couple of years before the Fair, and even then the price of the grapefruits was $5 per box. It was quite a luxury fruit, considering that would be $100 a box today.

The English bakery in the Manufactures Building introduced the scone to Americans. "Who ever attempted a British scone in this country or heard of one; but the British scone is now known to thousands and will be known to tens of thousands. It is a boon we must owe to Britain, along with the basic principles of our government," said a reporter in the *San Jose (Calif.) Mercury* in October 1904. He or she might have gotten a bit carried away about the universal popularity of the scone in the U.S. or its equality with the institution of democracy, but Britain did share one of its tasty treasures with us.

A farmer from a Texas County, Mo., town called Houston was about 90 years ahead of his time when he displayed a very rare food item — at least in this country — **ginseng**. Thomas Miland entered his gallon jar into the juried events and walked away with top prizes. It did not become popular then, but the *Post-Dispatch* reported that a "businessman offered him $50,000 for his acre of ginseng." So someone obviously thought it would become popular in the near future.

The Sacramento Valley, Calif., exhibitors displayed a fruit that very few people outside of California had ever seen — **the black or ripe olive**. The process of preserving the ripe olive had not yet been perfected; so very few bottles ever left California. What was produced only met the state's own consumption demands; so there was no supply left for the rest of the country. However, the fruit becoming known at the Fair probably gave Californians the needed boost to develop the preserving process.

The *National Fruit Growers Journal* informed its readers that never-seen-before varieties of **peaches and plums** were displayed at the Fair — Guinns, Annies, Williams, Texas Kings, and Poole peaches. Maybe they became popular eventually, but to the majority of fairgoers, peaches and plums by any other names were still peaches and plums!

Another "fruit" item may have gotten more notice. The National Ice Cartridge and Novelty Co. of New Jersey advertised its products with the slogan, "If you would 'cut the cotton' try a **fruit icicle**." It had three booths to demonstrate and sell its product. The sweetened liquid was frozen in a pliable tin tube, and dry-

Thomas Miland entered his gallon jar of ginseng into the juried events and walked away with top prizes. It did not become popular then, but the *Post-Dispatch* reported that a "businessman offered him $50,000 for his acre of ginseng."

mouthed fairgoers could heat the tube with their hands enough to push up the refreshing icicle. There is no prior history to cite on this item, but we do know that it went on to become what we know as a "Popsicle."

Then there were foods that did not even come close to being "preserved" through time. They may have been introduced at the Fair, but they were quickly and appropriately forgotten!

The Californians had an idea that was perhaps ahead of its time. They came up with what appears to have been the first **flavored coffees**. However, their choice of flavors seems, at worst, incongruous, and, at best, leaving something to be desired. Just imagine banana-and-prune-flavored coffee! There is no record of how well these went over, but they are certainly not on a Seattle's Best or Starbuck's list today.

> "If you would 'cut the cotton' try a fruit icicle."

If David Maxey wanted to use a nearby source of cream for his experiment, he could have visited the St. Charles Condensing Co.'s booth in the Agriculture building.
Courtesy Dr. Lyndon Irwin.

The world almost had an "instant smoothie" in 1904. Although David Maxey's display and contribution to the Fair did not rock the agricultural world (or probably even work), it was a "sort-of" first. The farmer from Aline, Okla., displayed a new way of feeding his melon crops. Adapting the familiar method of **sweetening melons** with bottled sugar water attached to the tendril of the fruit, Maxey used milk as the enhancing agent. The *Globe-Democrat* detailed the man's method in an article entitled, "Nurse Watermelons with Bottle to Fatten Them." "The fluid, he believes will act with the same effect upon the vegetable as [it does] upon the animal world ... his neighbors are watching the experiment with as much interest as the ingenious inventor himself. The possibilities," the reporter said, "of the scheme if successful are unlimitable [sic]." In post-Fair years, we have had to do our own mixing of cantaloupes and milk products. At least no one to date has picked a melon already filled with cottage cheese!

The Real Firsts

Without any stretch of the truth or imagination, there were foods or food-related items that did make their first appearance at the Fair and maintained some degree of popularity in history. However, to deflect any possible disappointment from the outset, there is no evidence that any foods or food-related items were *invented* between April 30 and December 1, 1904 — the months of the Fair. All had some history and some previous associations.

> … there is no evidence that any foods or food-related items were invented between April 30 and December 1, 1904 — the months of the Fair.

See if you can imagine this "first": "As one walks along he comes across a great variety of queer things to eat and drink. One of these is called **"Fairy Floss"** which is made of pure granulated sugar and looks like raw cotton. The sugar is melted in the center of a pan by electricity and thrown out centrifugally in a heated state and sold almost as fast as it was made," reported Orwin C. Painter to his *Baltimore American* readers in July 1904. Painter was talking about a relatively new confection first written about in 1900 and now known in this country as "cotton candy."

When fairgoers tasted Fairy Floss, they were hooked. Fairy Floss (named after very fine silk fringe threads) was rarely sold at fairs because the confection had to be cooked slowly over a stove. But two candy makers from Tennessee created a permanent association with cotton candy and fairs starting with the big Fair in St. Louis. They invented an electric Fairy Floss maker and introduced it at the Fair under the name of the Electric Candy Maker Co. The men packaged their creation in an ornately

This extremely rare collectible of the paper that covered three sides of a Fairy Floss box also shows the official seal of Norris B. Gregg, the director of concessions.
Courtesy Pat Villmer.

wrapped box, about the size of a Cracker Jack box today, and they reported to the Exposition that they sold about 70,000 boxes at 25 cents each!

"**Puffed Rice**, the cereal shot from a canon." Those words would later be the slogan for one of the true "first foods" seen at the Exposition. Fairgoers witnessed something entirely new when they saw eight real Spanish-American War type canons at the Quaker Oats exhibit shooting puffed rice out their barrels about every 50 minutes! The owner of the Anderson Puffed Rice Co., a subsidiary of Quaker Oats, had invented this method of puffing rice just the year before. The canons were heated to a temperature that made the rice explode to eight times its size. With proper fanfare, the canons were fired spewing the rice into the air around the exhibit. Freshly puffed rice was then caramelized, boxed, and sold at the company's booth. It must have been popular because the Louisiana and Texas Rice Kitchen jumped on the bandwagon and sold "puffed rice candy" for 5 cents, writing it in on its menu after the fact.

In an effort to lure the "working mom" and provide her with quick and nourishing meal options, the Joseph Campbell Preserve Co. added the cherubic faces of little children to its soup labels in early 1904. Ads on trolley cars in parts of New Jersey and Pennsylvania attracted female consumers to the convenience and healthfulness of the product. **The Campbell Kids** made their world premier a few months later at the Fair and have stayed around ever since.

This booth in the Quaker Oats Co.'s exhibit sold thousands of boxes of candied puffed rice, a confection introduced at the Fair (detail).

Courtesy, Missouri Historical Society, St. Louis.

In a Class of Its Own

But what about the ice cream cone? The crème de la crème of icons still stands as a solid candidate for having been invented and popularized by the masses of spring and summer visitors to St. Louis.

"Eating on the Pike is quite the fad if time is to be economized. The waffle cornucopia filled with ice cream or dainty French 'rose cakes' are enjoyed as we walk from one show to another," Mrs. F.M. Hicklin reported this to her fellow South Carolinians in a Columbus newspaper article in 1904. Oral histories from the 1960s to 1980s record plenty of stories about the first ice cream.

Here is the basic plot: A concessionaire at the Fair took a freshly made, waffle-like pastry called a "zalabia," curled it around a conical piece of wood, and then let it cool and harden. The result produced a firm, cone-shaped, waffle that the vendor then filled with ice cream.

But exactly who was this creative vendor? There are many contenders for title of ice cream cone inventor — Ernest Hamwi, Abe Doumar, David Avayou, the Menches brothers, and Nick and Albert Kabbaz, to name the most prominent. Whoever it was had to have been in cooperation with the Star Bottling Co., because it had the exclusive rights to ice cream at the Fair.

The International Association of Ice Cream Manufacturers credits Hamwi, a Lebanese immigrant, with taking his zalabias (invented much earlier in the Persian Gulf) and filling them with ice cream. After the Fair, he sold his waffle oven to J.P. Henckle, who started the Cornucopia Waffle Co. Hamwi went on to open the Missouri Cone Co. in 1910.

The family of Abe Doumar, a Syrian immigrant, is still pushing him into first place. He apparently did the same thing as Hamwi with the zalabia. Stories say he went at the business of marketing the cornucopia dainty on the Pike each evening, turning his 1-cent waffle into a 10-cent product by adding ice cream.

Avayou, a Turkish immigrant, is also credited with starting to serve ice cream in a waffle cone at the Fair. He claimed it was a French confection that he'd seen in Paris and that he'd just transported it to Fair. We know for sure that he went on to sell ice cream cones at a department store in Philadelphia.

Charles Menches and his brother were highly seasoned fair food vendors. The book, *Famous First Facts*, credits Menches and his brother with the introduction of the ice cream cone. This bumps Hamwi out of first place because he was only the maker of the zalabias, and the Menches brothers were supposedly the ones

One of the many ice cream cone machines patented in the years just after the 1904 World's Fair. The waffle cone was cooked and formed all in one process. These machines give credence to the theory that the cone was popularized during the Fair.

Louise Rice,
courtesy Chariton Co.
Historical Society Museum,
Salisbury, Mo.

who came up with the winning combination: ice cream in the zalabia cone. The Library of Congress website credits him with the invention. This much is true: The brothers started the Premium Ice Cream Cone and Candy Co. in Ohio right after the Fair.

Two other contenders for first place were nip and tuck with Hamwi because they worked in his booth. Nick and Albert Kabbaz — Syrian immigrants — claimed that they were the first to invent the idea of zalabia plus ice cream!

> The combination of ice cream and waffles had already been thought of and was called at that time an "ice cream sandwich."

Some facts about the ice cream cone:

1. In September 2003, Dairy Queen celebrated the birth of the ice cream cone by giving out complimentary cones, admitting that, by doing so, it might cause a meltdown of the 1904 legend. The company was celebrating the work of New Yorker, Italo Marchioney, who obtained U.S. patent No. 746,971 for an ice cream "cone" in December 1903. St. Louis Fair enthusiasts contend that his ice cream holder was not a cone at all, but rather a waffle "cup" with a flat bottom. It was meant to hold ice cream, but it was not a cone. Dairy Queen acknowledges the 1904 Fair as a significant event that made the ice cream cone popular.

2. The combination of ice cream and waffles had already been thought of and was called at that time an "ice cream sandwich." Concessionaire No. 121, who did not actually show up at the Fair, had earned the right to sell his combination. So ice cream sandwiches preceded the cone, but someone had to think of folding the waffles over to make the

This famous picture is the only known photo of any fairgoers eating a "cornucopia" at the Fair. Randolph, Mildred, Montague Jr., and their mother, Frances Lyon, enjoy the new sweet in front of one of the Pike concessions New York to the North Pole. This amusement was located just off the Amusement Strip.

Montague Lyon Collection, courtesy Missouri Historical Society, St. Louis.

cone-shaped ice cream holder we have grown to love!

3. We have at least one picture of people at the Fair eating ice cream cones. The photograph on the front cover of this book is the one most frequently reproduced. Although we don't know from which concessionaire on the Pike they got them, this much is certain: The family of Montague Lyon, a St. Louis lawyer, is enjoying ice cream cones in front of the New York to the North Pole amusement at the 1904 World's Fair. Randolph, Mildred, Montague, Jr., and their mother, Frances Lyon, were snapped by Mr. Lyon's "Exposition approved" camera in a rare moment of cultural transgression. Victorians did not think it was proper to eat in public.

4. We know that the Lyons weren't the only family to enjoy the cornucopias. A 1967 *Post-Dispatch* article quoted Mrs. Enid Locke Barnes as saying, "My family spent a week in 1904 at the St. Louis World's Fair. I remember distinctly eating an ice cream cone on the grounds and seeing a sort of thin round waffle cooked and rolled while hot into a cone shape. The ice cream melted somewhat and dripped from the hole in the bottom of the cone, but it was delicious. The cone was sweet and crisp and we ate it all. I was 11 and my sister was 8."

Food historians agree that it is doubtful, despite all the efforts of the candidates' descendants, that there will ever be proof of who was the first to invent the ice cream cone. Marchioney had a patent in 1903 for a waffle cup, and the other fellows went on in post-1904 years to develop patents and start ice cream cone companies of their own. Perhaps it was an idea whose time had come, and it was realized at the 1904 World's Fair in a big way! It was certainly the first time that large groups of people carried around their ice cream desserts and snacks in such a novel shape.

> Perhaps it was an idea whose time had come, and it was realized at the 1904 World's Fair in a big way!

Sarah Tyson Rorer's Philadelphia Gas Stove as pictured in her 1902 edition of Mrs. Rorer's New Cook Book.

Author's collection.

Sarah Tyson Rorer

Mrs. Rorer deserves a place among the "first" makers referred to in this chapter because she made two innovative contributions to food and food preparation. Although Mrs. Rorer did not invent the first gas stove, she did produce one that permitted the temperature to be regulated — a real first in its day. An ad appeared in the *Philadelphia Public Ledger* in May 1902 for "Mrs. S. T. Rorer's Philadelphia Gas Range" with a heat indicator for $16.50. Unfortunately, there is nothing written on exactly how she came to do this, but we can assume that, "Necessity is the mother of invention."

Mrs. Rorer's stove is still a highly prized collectible for antique stove dealers, but the result of another of her ideas is likely to be sitting in the kitchen pantry of most cooks around the world. While she was at the Chicago World's Fair in 1893, Mrs. Rorer wrote a letter to the gelatin entrepreneur Charles B. Knox, who was the father of the future orangeade concessionaire at the St. Louis Fair:

> "Dear Sir:
> May I suggest to you to granulate your Gelatine, and keep same up to its present high standard of quality? So many new recipes call for a small amount of Gelatine, and the ordinary household scales do not weigh less than an ounce, when frequently we need even an eighth of an ounce. I think you can readily understand what a convenience this form of Gelatine will be to the ordinary cook, who can readily measure it by tablespoonfuls or by teaspoonfuls.
>
> Yours very truly,
> Sarah Tyson Rorer"

On October 1, 1893, the form of the gelatin was changed from shredded to granulate. On the back cover of his publication, *Dainty Desserts for Dainty People*, Knox acknowledged Sarah Tyson Rorer and Mary Lincoln of the Boston Cooking School for suggesting this helpful change.

Mrs. Rorer's *World's Fair Souvenir Cook Book* included recipes using gelatin as well as ones that would have reflected some of the featured foods of the Fair. The following are all from her 1904 Fair cookbook, except the one for Hamburg Steak. That is taken from her 1902 classic, *Mrs. Rorer's New Cook Book*.

Peach Ice Cream
"Put a pint of cream on to boil in a farina boiler; when hot add ten ounces of sugar, and stir until dissolved. Take from the fire, add another pint of cream and when cold, freeze. Pare and mash a quart of peaches and stir them quickly into the frozen cream. Turn the crank rapidly for five minutes, then remove the dasher, repack the tub, cover, and stand away for two hours to ripen." (A farina boiler is a double boiler.)

Saratoga Potatoes

"Pare perfectly sound potatoes, cut them into thin slices, soak in cold water for thirty minutes. Dry them on a towel, and fry them a few pieces at a time in smoking hot lard. Cook carefully until a light brown and very crisp. Drain; put them in a colander on a soft piece of brown paper, dust with salt and place at the oven door a moment to dry."

(This recipe is from the same club that is credited with "inventing" the club sandwich!)

A Good Table Mustard

"Moisten two tablespoonfuls of corn starch with a little cold water, then add to it a half-pint of boiling water, stir until it boils, take it from the fire, and add two tablespoonfuls of tarragon vinegar, two teaspoonfuls of ground mustard, a level teaspoonful of salt, a dash of cayenne, a half-teaspoonful of cloves, and a level teaspoonful of cinnamon; keep closely covered."

Hamburg Steak

"[Use] 2 pounds of lean beef, 1 rounding teaspoonful of salt, 1 tablespoonful of grated onion, 1 saltspoonful of pepper. Purchase the upper portion of the round or the rump steak; trim off the fat and skin and put the meat twice through a meat chopper; add the pepper and onion, and form at once into small steaks, being careful to have them of even thickness. Place these on the broiler, broil over a slow fire for ten minutes. It takes longer to broil a Hamburg steak an inch thick than it does an ordinary steak of the same thickness. Dish on a heated plate, dust with salt, put a little butter on top of each and send at once to the table; or, they may have poured over them tomato sauce, or you may serve them with brown or sweet pepper sauce. Where broiling is out of the question, these may be pan-broiled."

Orange Bavarian Cream

"Cover a half-box of gelatine with a half-cup of cold water, and soak a half-hour. Thoroughly chill a pint of cream and whip it to froth … an eggbeater will do the work, and the froth may be skimmed off and placed on a sieve as fast as it comes to the surface. Add a cup of sugar to a pint of orange juice; stir until the sugar is dissolved. Place the gelatine over boiling water, and when it is dissolved add it to the orange juice, then add the whipped cream, stand the basin in pack of cracked ice, and stir carefully but constantly until the ingredients are thoroughly mixed and chilled, then turn in a mold and stand."

CHAPTER 11

Daily Specials

Each and every day the Fair offered a roster of specials. *The Daily Official Program* listed these occasions and directed visitors to the special parades, band concerts, and free souvenirs that accompanied the events. Every food vendor, restaurateur, and caterer's cash register rang a happier tune during these times because special events brought in more hungry people!

Courtesy Max Storm.

More than 100 associations held annual meetings at the Fair. Some associations made headlines the minute their attendees hit the turnstile, and what they did often brought even more recognition. The National Education Association's 50,000 members adopted their agenda for the year. The Democratic National Convention nominated its candidate who would run and lose against Theodore Roosevelt. Other groups, like the National Curio and Stamp Collectors and the National Association of Music Dealers, did not ever make the headlines, but they did draw a crowd.

The Exposition offered meeting rooms to associations for free, which was a wise marketing strategy on the Fair's part. The associations conducted their proceedings all day, and members were free to enjoy the Pike in the evening for dinner or entertainment. All the associations wanted to show their members a good time while they were in St. Louis and provided at least one banquet for their group. These dinners were served by restaurant caterers who tried to outdo not only themselves but also the other caterers on the grounds. Catering companies were proud to place their names on the souvenir menus for the evening banquets and knew the word would spread about a job well done — or not!

To orchestrate the events, the Exposition formed yet another committee — the Committee on Ceremonies. It was the "convention and visitors bureau" of the LPE, and all applications for a special event, meeting, or even a commemorative day passed the committee members' desks for approval.

Special Days

Any group could apply to have a special day named in its honor, particularly if it was holding its annual meeting on the fairgrounds. There was the Stenographers Day, the Council of Jewish Women's Day, and even the Rural Letter Carriers Day.

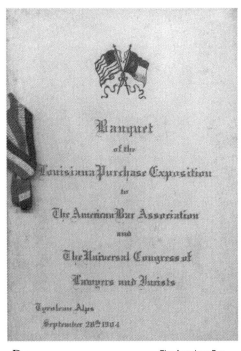

The Improved Order of Heptasophs Day probably caused a lot of fairgoers to open their *Daily Official Program* and say, "Huh?" If the Heptasophs and the other 50 fraternal orders and secret societies wanted anonymity, the Fair was hardly the place to preserve it!

There were also famous people days: for example, Lewis and Clark Day and Mark Twain Day. Helen Keller showed up for her day, and President Roosevelt showed up for his. LPE President Francis showed up every day, of course, but the last day was dedicated specially to him.

Colleges, states, and cities had their own days. Because so many groups applied for this special designation, the Committee on Ceremonies allowed more

The American Bar Association held one of the larger meetings at the Fair. The association held its main dinner in the Tyrolean Alps Restaurant.

Courtesy Max Storm.

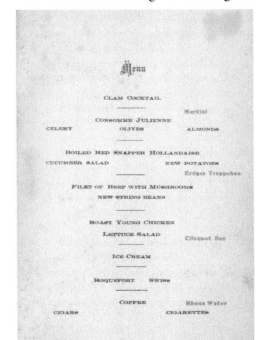

than one group to share a day. Perhaps it was a bit "prophetic" when New York Day and Apple Day got scheduled together. "Big Apple" might strike a familiar association with New York City today, but in 1904 the association would have been with Missouri. Because of the variety and numbers of apples it produced each year, Missouri had earned the title, "Land of the Big Red Apple."

Special Food Events

There were days dedicated to food as well as to people and groups. Apple Day and World's Fair Orange and Flower Day were two of the biggest food-related events. Much like today's "hat day" or "bat day" at the ballpark, World's Fair visitors received giveaways representative of the featured item. Thirty thousand oranges passed into the hands of visitors to the Sacramento, Calif., exhibit between the hours of 1 and 5 p.m. on Orange and Flower Day. At one time, the line for the free fruit was 1,000 feet long. It took six men more than an hour to clear the area around the exhibit of orange peelings and the tissue paper covers required by the Department of Exhibits. In some areas, the sweepers reported that the piles of debris were nearly a foot high!

There were a number of "Masters" events held at the Fair that year, but none of them had anything to do with golf! There was the Master Butchers of America Day, the Brew Masters Day, and the Master Bakers Day. One day overshadowed all of these in attendance and recognition, however. Farmers Day was Sept. 15, 1904 — the same as St. Louis Day. It is remembered as having the highest recorded attendance for the seven months of the Fair, with more than 400,000 people attending. Since visitors did not register their reason for attending the Fair, we cannot know for sure which designation drew the crowd. But agricultural journals had been encouraging farmers to come to the Fair for nearly a year before their big day. The *Tennessee Farmer* was a little ambitious in its October 1903 prediction that 5 million farmers would show up on Farmers Day!

When the five hundred members of the National Brewers Association and their wives attended a banquet at the Tyrolean Alps, the estimated wealth in the room was $500 million!

When the five hundred members of the National Brewers Association and their wives attended a banquet at the Tyrolean Alps, the estimated wealth in the room was $500 million! After the banquet, members of the association read the annual reports. The *Republic* recorded: "[It has been] reported that while there had been a great mass of literature published in the last year arguing the bad effects of beer drinking, it was clear that beer was a nutrition rather than otherwise, and that the amount of alcohol it contains was not enough to be injurious." It was certainly important for *their* health and wealth to think that!

The menu of food-related associations holding their meetings at the Fair read like a household grocery list:

Pretzel Fraternity of America
Apple Shippers Association

Apple Growers Congress of America
Brewers Association of the United States
Bread Bakers National Association
Poultry Association of America
Nut Growers National Association
National Dairymen Association
Agricultural Press League
Pure Food Congress
Vegetarian Congress

Some of the meetings were small — just an evening banquet. Others lasted for a full week. All of them brought interesting people to the Fair, and the Fair provided a unifying experience for specialists and special-interest groups.

Special Meetings

The multitude of congress attendees all had to eat at the Fair. The caterers kept them well fed while their associations kept them well informed.

The largest special events were the congresses bringing thousands of people from all over the country or the world to St. Louis for their meetings. The largest congress was the National Education Association Convention already mentioned. Other congresses included the International Press Congress, the Congress for the Deaf, the Sunday Rest Congress, and the Peace Congress. The multitude of congress attendees all had to eat at the Fair. The caterers kept them well fed while their associations kept them well informed.

One of the most impressive special meetings was a banquet held in the Tyrolean Alps and hosted by Edward and Sons, a brokerage house in St. Louis. The firm invited the "Post and Flagg" association, whose members included 25 American millionaires. The food was catered by the Alps and the decorations were early 20th-century "Martha Stewart." The dining room was decorated with evergreens, and, in the center of the table, was an illuminated reproduction of one of the large Wall Street banks. A miniature railroad track encircled the center of the table, with each guest's plate representing a train station. The stock market's bear and bull were even present — in live versions right there in the dining room!

Another special meeting honored someone not in the room and not even alive. Fifteen years before the Fair, Henry Shaw, the great botanist, philanthropist, and designer of the famous Shaw's Garden, had died, and his will had provided that $1,000 a year be used for a banquet in his honor. In 1904, the Annual Shaw Banquet was held at the World's Fair during the most prestigious of congresses — the Congress of Arts and Sciences. About 300 scientists attended the science banquet and remembered Shaw's work.

There were also meetings on a much smaller scale to meet more intimate needs. Families had their reunions at the Fair, and even had "days" named for them — the Kingsbury Family Reunion Day and the Paxon Family Reunion Day. Schools, too, arranged for events to take place at the Fair. The local Christian Brothers College had its high school graduation on the fairgrounds, and the Yale Alumni Club socialized on the veranda of the Tyrolean Alps.

The Exhibitors Association held a luncheon here in the Palace of Horticulture after its exhibits had been inspected by the Exposition's official inspectors, May 15, 1904.

Emil Boehl, courtesy Missouri Historical Society, St. Louis.

Sarah Tyson Rorer

Mrs. Rorer had an interesting philosophy about hosting special events within the home, for example, a dinner party. She advised that all upsets or mishaps around serving a meal when company came for dinner could be avoided if the housewife or hired help would "serve food every day in the year in the best and most attractive manner possible. Follow the same routine," she said, "each day, and serve the family in the same manner as guests, otherwise you may be mortified when the guests are present." She admonished her listeners to forgo special sets of dishes just for company and thought the family deserved equally special treatment.

Mrs. Rorer's *World's Fair Souvenir Cook Book* does acknowledge special events, however, and offers bills of fare for major holidays as well as for more unusual occasions such as these:

LUNCH FOR TENNIS PARTY
Tongue Sandwiches, Olives, Almonds
Deviled Eggs, Sardines
Water Crackers
Lemonade

LENTEN DINNERS
Bisque of Oysters
Fish Cutlets, Cream Sauce
Boiled Cod, Shrimp Sauce
Potatoes
Lettuce Salad, French Dressing
Wafers, Cheese
Coffee

AN EMERGENCY DINNER OF CANNED GOODS
Cream of Tomato Soup
Broiled Salt Mackerel, Parsley Sauce
Lyonnaise Potatoes
Timbale of Macaroni, Cream Sauce
French Omelet with Peas
Lettuce Salad, French Dressing
Wafers, Cheese
Canned Fruit
Coffee

Here are some recipes from Mrs. Rorer's cookbook that would be fitting for special events today:

Veal Cutlet

"The usual method of dipping a thick cutlet into egg and crumbs, and then frying slowly in lard is abominable. But if the cutlet be cut as thin as a knife blade, blanched by pouring over it boiling water, then dried, dipped, and fried quickly in nice veal suet, it will be both palatable and comparatively wholesome."

Oyster Sauce

"Boil twenty-five oysters in their own liquor for one minute, stirring continually; drain, put the liquor back on the fire; add one cup of cream or milk; rub one tablespoonful of butter and two of flour to a smooth paste, and stir into the boiling liquor until it thickens. Chop the oysters into dice, add them to the sauce, season with salt and pepper, and take from the fire. This will curdle if boiled after adding the oysters. Serve with poultry and boiled fish."

Broiled Fillet of Beef

"Cut the fillet into pieces one inch thick. Mix together two tablespoonfuls of melted butter and one of lemon juice. Moisten the meat carefully with this mixture and stand in a cold place for one hour or longer, then place them in a wire broiler, and broil five minutes over a clear fire turning the broiler 10 times. Serve with salt, pepper, and melted butter or with tomato or mushroom sauce."

Main Events

Every day the Fair was the scene of hundreds of celebrations. Even the *Daily Official Program* could not list all the dedications, special receptions, state, foreign, and government events, and honorary banquets. Many of them were special interest events, but others had more universal appeal. There were three that got a lot of press during the fall and winter of 1904 and captured the hearts of many. One honored a person and his office, President Theodore Roosevelt, the second celebrated a national holiday tradition, Thanksgiving, and the third lauded a piece of fruit! The last will not seem so unusual once the turn-of-the-century reverence for the apple is explained.

Apple Honors

"… this combination of baked apples is the one dish that will prove healthful to all sufferers from indigestion of all types."

An apple a day kept more than the doctor away, according to many apple advocates in 1904. It might also keep the law enforcer and the social worker away! Not only could the apple keep one healthy in body, but it could also mend a broken spirit and prevent societal disorders as well. "Apples will make a man bright, moral and virtuous," said a St. Louis man in the March 1903 *Modern Grocer*. "It would be cheaper to give every boy a full allowance of apples than to try young desperados."

Apples were so highly thought of that they had their own special department in the Horticulture Building — the pomology department. Its superintendent was Professor John T. Stinson, whose research into apples as a cure for drinking and smoking received a lot of endorsement at the time.

Harriet MacMurphy, who would not commit herself on exactly what she would serve dyspeptics at the Fair, came out strongly in favor of apples: "… yes, baked apples. That is one of the dishes I most strongly recommend. They are stuffed with almonds and filled with whipped cream. There are at least a half-dozen kinds of dyspeptics. But this combination of baked apples is the one dish that will prove healthful to all sufferers from indigestion of all types."

Apple Displays

Thousands of plates of apples were constantly before the public eye in the Horticulture Building. Thanks to the successful experiment with refrigeration, it was possible to have apples from the 1903 crops displayed on the first day of the Fair. In fact, Missouri's Guano apples had been picked in 1901 and 1902. The combination of natural hardiness and cold storage made them still fit for the Fair.

As with every exhibit at the Fair, there were rules to follow. Fruits in cold storage had to have inner wrappers made of "soft paper," i.e., tissue paper or blank newsprint, and outer wrappers for which "a paraffin paper was most desirable." The apples had to be displayed on standard plates, designated by the Department of Exhibits, which were made and sold by the Ohio China Co. This was done not only for appearance but also to assist the visitor's eye when making comparisons among apples. Collectors can find the off-white china with the LPE symbol and the green line around the rim in flea markets across the country.

Like all other displays of food, the apple exhibitors had to keep them fresh and attractively presented. West Virginia's S.W. Moore kept 1,000 plates of apples on display constantly in the state's horticultural booth, and his cold storage unit was full of replacements. So many apples came to the Fair from West Virginia that year that the local papers reported a shortage of apples for the people back home. Not yet a state, the territory of Oklahoma made an impressive display of 500 plates of apples, and the October 1904 issue of the *Apple Specialist* complimented the territory on its productivity in fewer than 10 years of apple cultivation

Visitors did a double take when they passed one Nebraska apple grower's display. When the fruit was still young, he had cut out of paper the names of the apples and

Colorado had an impressive exhibit of apples in the Palace of Horticulture. Here they are displayed on the Ohio China Co. plates required by the Division of Exhibits.

Courtesy Dr. Lyndon Irwin.

pasted them on each one. After the sun turned the rest of the apple bright red and the paper was removed, the name was still clearly visible.

Apple Day

All of this attention culminated in the final months of the Fair when the new crop of apples ripened in the major apple-producing states. The Exposition assigned a "day" to any of those states promising to distribute apples. Arkansas got one, and, according to the September issue of the *Farmer and Stockman Journal*, distributed 10 train carloads to apple-loving visitors.

October 4 was the official "Apple Day" for the whole fair, and the Horticulture Building was the center of the celebration. The distribution of apples was such a huge undertaking that states arranged for special teams to give out the fruit. The *Republic* reported that, "Forty girls, selected for their charm and beauty (and each one from a different participant state) gave away apples from 1,250 barrels organized by the exhibitors." The article likened the 40 girls to an army. Their "general" was Florence B. Appleby, who was in fact chosen for this role because of her last name. The enemies were cigars, beer, whiskey, and other liquors. "Instead of shrapnel, bomb shells and thousands of whizzing bullets," said the *Republic*, "the attacking army will use smiles, winning ways and — apples." The army of girls had, "Stop smoking, eat apples," as its battle cry!

Nebraska's apple display had a unique surprise for the visitors. The name of the apple had been "imprinted" during the ripening process.
Courtesy Dr. Lyndon Irwin.

"Forty girls, selected for their charm and beauty (and each one from a different participant state) gave away apples from 1,250 barrels organized by the exhibitors."

Thanksgiving

By 1904, Thanksgiving had been a national holiday for more than 50 years, and people might have been expected to stay at home. But it was business as usual at the Fair, and, despite the chilly early winter temperatures, people came through the turnstiles for a once-in-a-lifetime Thanksgiving dinner, if not to see the Fair!

Fair Japan Restaurant, for example, served a traditional Thanksgiving meal that cost $1 and included soups, relishes, oysters, turkey, dressing, cranberry sauce, corn, sweet potatoes, and, of course, apple pie, mince pie, and ice cream.

The Board of Lady Managers held two large Thanksgiving dinners at its building to accommodate the relief shifts of the Jefferson Guard. The Indian School prepared a Thanksgiving dinner and invited native peoples — the Apaches, Pueblos, Navajos, and Kickapoos from North America, and the Patagonians, Ainus, and Pigmies from the foreign nations. Many of their children, however, were at the most acclaimed celebration of the day — Thanksgiving at the Model Playground.

The event captured the headlines of many newspapers around the world because it was

On any day during the Fair, the Model Playground was filled with children from all over the world.
Courtesy Dr. Lyndon Irwin.

more than a feast. It was a promise of hope for the future of mankind to have 326 children representing many of the nations at the Fair come together for the Thanksgiving celebration.

Donations had poured in from individuals and companies to help finance the large event. The Board of Lady Managers contributed the most — $100. Native St. Louisans will recognize the names of other contributors — the Stix, Baer, and Fuller Co., the Scruggs, Vandervoort and Barney Co., as well as the May Co. They sent $15 each. The commissioners to the Fair from Haiti, Peru, Denmark, and the Philippines had made contributions as well. One contributor just signed "a friend" on the 50-cent contribution.

Other donations came in kind. The National Biscuit Co. donated cakes, Pillsbury baked the rolls, Sprague Deli donated pumpkin pies, and the St. Louis Dairy Co. provided the ice cream. The Inside Inn donated the hams, and the Tyrolean Alps brought forth a "hamper of provisions." C.A. Windmueller provided bags of popcorn, and the Louisiana and Texas Rice Kitchen put rice on the table. Other companies and individuals donated the centerpieces and the tables and chairs. The Exposition, through its Bureau of Music, donated the band and Bandmaster Weil for the event.

Mrs. Hirshfield had sent invitations to 44 nations, and half of them responded. The only requirement for the children was that they were old enough to sit at the table, eat turkey, and not be over the age of 15. One of the most unusual guests was Lomo, a Pygmy, who was the right age and who was the size of a 12-year-old, but who already had two wives and a number of children himself!

Twelve automobiles went throughout the fairgrounds at about 11 a.m. and picked up the children. Each driver had a manifest with the children's names and would ask the name of each child, check it off the list, and then motion the child into the car. The Nov. 25 issue of the *Globe-Democrat* included a touching story: "Attendants were flustered by the strange names and one attendant forgot his own name when a young Igorot asked him [the driver] his name." For people who were referred to as "uncivilized," this was a courtesy not necessarily found in all societies.

Parents from all nations had gotten their children ready in their best clothes and probably reminded them to eat and behave properly. Their children were the ambassadors to the world that afternoon. There was no national monopoly on the parental love, pride, and concern for the child who stepped into the cars and rode to the gathering. Many of the parents followed to join the 20,000 spectators who stood outside the fences of the Model Playground. Chief Sitting Bear of the Sioux Indians and his squaw brought their 4-year-old son themselves and escorted him into the play area. The planning committee had arranged for games of amusement representing different cultures.

> Parents from all nations had gotten their children ready in their best clothes and probably reminded them to eat and behave properly.

As the time for the meal came, the band began a march, and the children formed a double column marching twice around the playground following the band. The *Globe-Democrat* reported that, "The little Negrito girl [from the Philippines] in a pink-checkered gingham dress looked twice into the eyes of a little boy from the Boer country [in South Africa]. Then she slipped her hand into his

and fell into line." The children were allowed to choose their dinner partners. "The clear-eyed daughter of the Cheyenne Chieftain had for her partner at dinner a daughter of the far North [Esquimaux], clad in her bearskin robe with a bright-colored ribbon tying the braid of her dark hair. After taking their places in the open pavilion where the tables had been set," the *Globe-Democrat* reported, "the children sat spellbound for a while as they eyed the white tablecloths, floral arrangements, china and glassware. Many had never seen such place settings before."

The most prominent people to visit the children's feast were Fair President David Francis and Canadian Premier Sir Wilfred Laurier and their wives. The Dorr and Zeller caterers donated the 110-person wait staff for the children's meal, but the dignitaries could not resist assisting the children, too. Even Mrs. Francis removed her gloves and helped the young guests cut up their turkey.

The children heard speeches from the mayor and dignitaries. The Honorable Frederick A. Betts, a national commissioner for the World's Fair and the chairperson of the event, was probably the wisest in merely saying hello and expressing his desire that the children have a good time. He had already won their hearts at an earlier event that year when he invited 1,600 children to his birthday party, where he and his wife helped serve cake and ice cream.

"The children sat spellbound for a while as they eyed the white tablecloths, floral arrangements, china and glassware. Many had never seen such place settings before."

The children consumed 24 turkeys, 10 hams, and 15 gallons of ice cream. By dessert, some of the children's refinement began to wear off. One Moros child (a Philippine native) by the name of Fancondu wore a bright red silk suit and turban. He eyed the pumpkin pie critically for a minute, saw a waiter, and then jumped on the chair. "Hey," he called holding the pie by the top of the crust, "What this mean?"

Reporters observed that the Eskimo and Pygmy children enjoyed eating the ice cream, and some even asked for the recipe to give to their parents. The Moros, however, were shivering from the cold dish and pronounced it "impossible." A woman bystander suggested to the children that they run in the sun a bit to warm up. The children left the table, went into the sun, but never returned.

The children managed to show their respect and appreciation with rounds of loud applause for the planners. During the meal, someone asked them if they would like this kind of food in their countries, and all the children cheered a resounding "Yes." In the end they participated as best they could in the *Star Spangled Banner* and *America the Beautiful* played by Weil's band. As the children were escorted to their parents or to Exposition cars, the Blanke-Wenneker Candy Co. of St. Louis gave each child a bag of candy, and the Connecticut Commission provided a souvenir toy. The adults were pleased and thankful that all went well. Even the event that followed a few short days later would not overshadow this unique experience of a united world.

President Theodore Roosevelt's Visit

President Theodore Roosevelt and his presidential party arrived on the Saturday after Thanksgiving, Nov. 26, which had been designated "President's Day." "Teddy" Roosevelt was one of the most colorful presidents of all times. Just three weeks earlier he had been elected to his own term of office after serving the final three years of William McKinley's.

Secret Service men trailed Roosevelt throughout his visit to St. Louis, and there was heavy guard around W.H. Thompson's house on Lindell Avenue, where the Roosevelts stayed. What had happened at the 1901 Pan-American World's Fair in Buffalo, N.Y., was very fresh in the national memory and certainly was uppermost in the minds of those who had planned the Exposition. An anarchist had shot McKinley as he left a reception to attend a music concert, and he had died eight days later. The Secret Service was not about to let anything happen to Roosevelt.

It seems as though the threat did not deter him at all from enjoying everything the Fair had to offer. In fact, it seems fitting to refer to Roosevelt with his nickname, "Teddy," when describing his behavior. He "attacked" the Fair with a child-like enthusiasm a personality trait he exhibited in all his endeavors. He might have been saving time for sightseeing when he agreed to visit the Fair only if his hosts would refrain from making speeches in his honor — especially at dinners and banquets.

President Theodore Roosevelt and his wife, Edith, took great delight in the Fair during their visit in November. He preferred visiting to speech making, but here he addressed the crowd on November 26.

Courtesy Laura Brandt.

Teddy certainly had his favorite interests and visited those first. The North Dakota Commission brought his former hunting cabin from their state and rebuilt it in the North Dakota section of the Agriculture Building. Like his sons, he was anxious to visit the Philippine reservation — but perhaps for different reasons. Roosevelt had led the Rough Riders to victory over the Spanish in Cuba during the Spanish-

American War, and the Phillipines were part of the spoils of this war.

When the president visited the Puerto Rico exhibit, the attendants presented him with a cup of black Puerto Rican coffee, several boxes of their choice cigars, and a dozen large sacks of their best beans. When reporters later queried the president about his favorite beverage at the Fair, he replied that he most enjoyed the Puerto Rican coffee sipped in the San Juan exhibit of the Agricultural Building.

Fireworks began the evening festivities, and the Roosevelts were escorted to the main dining room of the Tyrolean Alps for dinner. Luchow and Faust, the managers and owners, had set 600 place settings for the guests. Forty-eight people sat at a long table decorated with La France roses and electric lights with varicolored shades. Above the orchestra were flags from all the participating countries, as well as the Exposition flag. Red, white, and blue bunting hung from the pillars. American Beauty roses were entwined in the balconies. Everywhere there were flowers and lights. Even an illuminated likeness of the president hung over his table with the lighted message, "Welcome, our President."

All the Fair officials and their wives were invited to the party. State and foreign commissioners also were invited, as were their wives. The Board of Lady Managers (and we can assume their husbands, too), the governors, and foreign dignitaries all received invitations to honor the president. He arrived at 8:20 p.m. with the playing of the *Star Spangled Banner.* According to the *World's Fair Bulletin* of December 1904, "Guests waved their handkerchiefs and napkins in the air to enthusiastic cheers of 'Hurrah for Roosevelt.' "

> "Guests waved their handkerchiefs and napkins in the air to enthusiastic cheers of 'Hurrah for Roosevelt.' "

He entered with the first lady, who wore pastel blue chiffon, velvet, and Irish lace. Alice wore pink chiffon and lace with diamonds — not the blue gown popularized in the song later written for her. All the diners were expected to be in formal attire, according to the official announcement from the Exposition management. Men were to be in evening dress and women in high-neck or reception gowns with hats. They all partook of the splendid meal planned for them.

Reporters from the *Republic* commented that "President Roosevelt seemed to enter thoroughly into the spirit of the occasion and there was every evidence to show that no one enjoyed the affair in a keener manner than did he. More than once in the evening did the President's countenance show that grin so familiar to the people of the United States.

MENU

Blue Points, Mignonette.
Olivette, Wurzburger Ofbrau.
Soup, Columbia.
Celery.   Radishes.   Almonds.
Salmon Soufflé, Admiral.
Caseler Hitzlay.
Julienne Potatoes.
Trarbacher, Schlossber.
Medallion of Beef, Louisiana.
Risotto with Truffles.
Pommery and Greno.
Quail, Hunter Style.
Salad, Oyster Bay.   Appollinaris.
Biscuit Glacé, Fantaisie.
Demi Tasse.   Cigars.

Then when the band played *Yankee Doodle*, the president beat time with his hands, but when *Dixie* was the tune he counted time with even greater zest and was seen to pound the table with his fist in approval."

Francis reflected the sentiments of many Americans in his after-dinner remarks, when he said, "the verdict of this November [1904 presidential election] was the result of various causes (laughter), and one of the potential factors in that result, if not by far the ruling one, was the personality of the successful candidate (applause)."

Roosevelt's personality was revealed in many ways at the

One of the Eastern correspondents called out one more question to the president: Had he enjoyed his visit? Smiling, he declared, "Why, my boy, I've had the time of my life!"

Butter sculpture of Theodore Roosevelt in the dairy display at the Palace of Agriculture.
Courtesy Yvonne Suess.

Fair, but one particularly charming display came while viewing one of the ubiquitous butter sculptures in the Agriculture Building. When he saw the sculpture of himself, reporters covering "the Roosevelt story" overheard a comment he made to his wife. After looking at the statue, he turned, smiled broadly at Edith, and asked, "Do I really look like that?"

At one minute after midnight on Monday, Nov. 28, the president and his entourage boarded the train for the 1,000-mile trip back to the White House. Adhering to contemporary American values, they did not travel on Sunday the 27th. While everyone was settling in, the president came back to thank the city police officers, the detectives, and the Secret Service for their work during his stay. As he turned around to board the train car, he looked one last time at the shadowy view of the fairgrounds. One of the Eastern correspondents called out one more question to the president: Had he enjoyed his visit? Smiling, he declared, "Why, my boy, I've had the time of my life!"

Sarah Tyson Rorer

The successful Sarah Tyson Rorer was a familiar face to most Americans.

Author's collection.

Mrs. Rorer's contribution to cookery has been considered a *main event* in the culinary history of the last 150 years. In 1972, James Beard dedicated his *James Beard's American Cookery* to "my favorite great ladies of the American kitchen." The short list of nine women included Mrs. Rorer.

A popular history of American cookery, *The Everlasting Pleasure* (1956), names Mrs. Rorer's cooking school and her demonstrations as one of the most important influences on American cooks and cookery. A 1947 article in the *Journal of the American Dietetic Association* claimed that, "Mrs. Rorer, who was a true scientist and made her craft a fine art, qualifies best as the predecessor of the modern dietician." There is no doubt, then, that she herself was a main event.

Here are recipes from her *World's Fair Souvenir Cook Book*, which pick up some of the flavors of this chapter's "main events."

Preserved Cranberries

"Put one pound of granulated sugar and a half-pint of water on to boil. Boil two minutes, skim, add one quart of cranberries, cover the saucepan and stand it on the back part of the range to heat slowly for two hours. They must not boil or the skins will break. These are very nice to serve with roasted fowl or turkey."

Apple Pudding Sauce

"Pare, core and stew four tart apples. When done, press them through a sieve, add to them the grated yellow rind and juice of one lemon and sufficient sugar to make them palatable. Add one ounce of butter and the well-beaten whites of two eggs. Serve cold, with dumplings or bread pudding."

Pumpkin Custard

"Pare and cut a Kershaw pumpkin into pieces about an inch square; put these into a porcelain-lined sauce pan, with just enough water to prevent burning. Stew slowly until tender, about a half-hour, then press through a colander. To every half-pint of pumpkin, add a piece of butter the size of a walnut, and a quarter-teaspoonful of salt. Mix and stand aside until cold. When cold, put in one pint of good milk, a half-teaspoonful of ground mace, the same of ground cinnamon, one teaspoonful of ground ginger, one cup of sugar and four well-beaten eggs. This quantity will make three large or four medium-sized pies."

Creamed Fish

"Pick into small pieces one pint of cold cooked fish, put one table-spoonful of flour, when mixed add one pint of milk, stir continuously until it boils, add one teaspoonful of salt and a saltspoonful of pepper. Mix the fish carefully with the sauce and turn into a shallow baking-dish or into individual dishes. Sprinkle the top with stale breadcrumbs and brown in the oven.

(Salt spoons were used with the individual salt cellar at each diner's place. A saltspoonful equalled a little more than a pinch.)

Food Fights and Other Disputes at the Fair

Say that the hot dog, the hamburger, and iced tea were not "invented" at the World's Fair and you might get into a verbal brawl with some native St. Louisans. But such a disagreement is tame compared to some of the disputes that went on before, during, and after the Fair.

> It may be hard to believe that a "neutral" topic like food could cause such major problems, but when profit, pride, or production issues entered into the mix, many people reached the "boiling point."

Not everyone thought things at the Fair were fair. From the beginning, the LPE Co. planned for everything from simple complaints to lawsuits, from petty violations to fraud and bribery, and it ended up having some of each. A hundred years of evolution make some of these food fights seem silly or insignificant, but, to the parties involved in 1904, they were serious issues, and simple statements could become "fighting words." Disagreements relating to food came from the vendors, concessionaires, the military, LPE stockholders, and World's Fair personnel. It may be hard to believe that a "neutral" topic like food could cause such major problems, but when profit, pride, or production issues entered into the mix, many people reached the "boiling point."

Preparation Pressures

During the preparation years, 1901 and 1902, there were already numerous "battles" about the Fair. Many women's groups were as adamant about maintaining propriety on the Pike as the Women's Christian Temperance Union was about alcohol. There was no rest from discussions with the Sabbatarians about Sunday closings; and there were ceaseless requests from the Anti-Cigarette League to snuff out the use of tobacco inside the fairgrounds.

A significant hubbub followed when Director of Exhibits Frederick Skiff decreed that male exhibitors and concessionaires must wear coats at the exhibits. Assured that the Board of Lady Managers was behind this, a gathering of male exhibitors went to the ladies and argued that to work in shirtsleeves was more suitable for the St. Louis heat. Skiff got involved and eventually announced to the Concessionaires Association that, "the spirit of the law, not the letter of law, needed to be observed" in this situation. And so the men worked in their "shirtwaists," their long-sleeved, buttoned shirts.

Sometimes the Exposition leadership saw a potential for trouble and headed it off at the pass. Director of Works Taylor noticed that the building plans for the military mess hall had the structure right next-door to the Board of Lady Managers' building. He had the engineers relocate the building somewhere else just about the time Mrs. Daniel Manning and the Board of Lady Managers were gathering to protest the construction.

The Amusement Section of the Central Trades and Labor Union averted some potentially sticky food fights by proposing that the concessionaires enter into an agreement with them because they had set wages for bartenders, waiters and waitresses, and cooks. Therefore, concessionaires would not have to deal with requests for raises, walkouts, or union-sanctioned strikes. The labor union had its conditions, however. All union employees were to receive free admission to the World's Fair and all the paid concessions. Bartenders got an extra perk: a per diem for boat excursions and picnics! The best cooks got $120 a month or more. Waiters received $15 a week, and the ones working on commission got $1 a day plus $1.20 worth of checks (prepaid coupons to be used throughout the Fair) for $1. Waitresses received $11.40 a week with no perks except the one clearly stipulated by the union: every union worker ate for free. Each concessionaire was free to accept or reject the union's offer.

> All union employees were to receive free admission to the World's Fair and all the paid concessions.

Breaches of Contract

The greatest number of serious food fights was between the LPE Co. and the concessionaires and contractors. Because running a concession involved a legal agreement between the concessionaire and the LPE Co., many food fights concerned a breach of contract. Law firms hated to see the Fair end because business had been so good during those months!

The Exposition Water Co., which supplied the water for the water slot machines, sued the LPE Co. for $63,000 in damages, claiming that other vendors were able to market water in places too close to their stands, so that they were only able to sell one-half of the contracted amount. The Star Bottling Co., which sold soda, soft drinks, and ice cream, sued the company for the same reason, saying that too many other soda fountain vendors could sell the items for which the Star Bottling Co. had an "exclusive" contract.

This menu from the German Wine Restaurant displays the suggestion for diners to check their bill before paying.
Courtesy Max Storm.

The LPE Co., in turn, brought fines and penalties for what it believed was a breach of contract on part of the concessionaires. Mrs. McCready of the American Inn on the Model Street was held responsible for being late with her $5,700-a-month payment to the company. Whenever a restaurateur or concessionaire was delinquent with a payment, the bureau sent a team of "restaurant checkers" in to enforce the Exposition's restaurant system; that system included a complicated process of catching dishonest waiters who were manipulating the checks in their favor. We don't know if Mrs. McCready was the victim of her wait staff, but the Old Parliament House Restaurant tried to avoid the problem for both proprietor and guest by printing a warning on its menu: "Before paying the waiter see that your check is punched correctly."

The most famous person to have a food fight with the LPE Co. was Adolphus Busch, the brewer. Busch was a stockholder in both the LPE Co. and the Tyrolean Alps, and was a huge draw in bringing stockholders to the LPE Co. Busch said that the LPE Co. discriminated against the Luchow-Faust Restaurant Co., which owned the Tyrolean Alps, and that the $50,000 the LPE Co. said that it owed was preposterous. Although not withdrawing his stock holdings, Busch withdrew from any involvement in the management of the Louisiana Purchase Exposition of 1904. This time the committee did not let the reputation of a person affect the integrity of its decision. Regardless of the consequences, it held that Luchow-Faust owed $50,000.

Loss of Income

The concessionaires were businessmen and women who knew the basics of profit very well. Money coming in needed to exceed money going out, and they monitored every expense and any potential threat to income.

When restaurant concessionaires who also were caterers complained that too many outside caterers from St. Louis were getting too much of the banquet and reception business, "The Committee [on Concessions] voted that Mr. Gregg [director of concessions] should use his influence to have state and foreign commissioners use concession caterers for their requirement." It helped the cause of the caterers when word got around that, on June 11, 1904, one of downtown catering companies didn't show up at the annual convention of the Travelers Protective Association, and 10,000 traveling salesmen had to fend for themselves!

The Model Poultry Farm made a formal complaint to the Committee on Concessions, saying that 500 of its 4,000 chickens refused to hatch their eggs. Farm management claimed that the cause of this un-chicken-like behavior was the stress that they were under. The birds had to listen to the volleys of gunfire and cannon fire between the British and the Boers, who were re-enacting the Boer War. Because the concessions could not be moved, and the mock killing was essential to historical authenticity, the World's Fair management said that the chickens would have to roll over easy and produce the eggs despite the noisy conditions!

The concessions that had tobacco privileges complained to the committee that they were experiencing a loss of income because fewer fairgoers were smoking. The Anti-Cigarette League would have liked to take credit for the decline in smoking at the Fair, but it was actually by order of the Exposition that, because of the fire hazard, smoking was allowed only in restaurants, cafes, and a very few other locations. According to the July 21 issue of the *Republic*: "The latest salutation to be heard among the Exposition grounds was, 'Have you taken the smoke cure?' ... dozens of men who were chronic users of the weed had confessed to a complete cure since the opening of the Exposition."

The World's Fair Restaurant Men's Association complained that the LPE Co. charged too many fees and that the association already was giving 25 percent of its gross receipts to the Exposition. Specifically, it wanted its suppliers to have free admission to the Fair when the suppliers made deliveries. Association members claimed that the suppliers passed the additional cost on to them, and so they were compelled either to raise prices in their restaurants or lose money. The Restaurant Men's Association also asked for the removal of another tax, which charged the restaurateur 50 cents an hour every time a delivery person was escorted to the restaurant for a drop-off. Both taxes were removed.

Theft and Bribery

There were 100 protests over the selection of the famous Yale Coffee, whose maker was accused of brewing up a scheme to pay off jurors at the coffee competition. The accusations proved to be accurate.

Although the Jefferson Guard had been hired to protect the treasures of the world housed in the Fair's exposition halls, it also protected the real assets of the concessionaires and the LPE Co. in general. The souvenir hunters were the toughest to catch for the Jefferson Guard. Not unlike some honeymooners who manage to take the hotel's monogrammed towels as souvenirs, the 1904 visitors did similar things that caused the exhibitors loss of profit. Within a two-week period, one of the coffee exhibitors lost a dozen coffee cups and two dozen souvenir spoons with the various World's Fair buildings engraved on them.

The Jefferson Guard got involved in its own dispute at one point. Its 2 a.m. shift could not find any place to eat because the food concessionaire "cooks refused to make coffee or cook eggs after midnight. They declared that nothing could induce them to take up the rolling pin or cookbook." When the majority of the night shift threatened to resign, the Exposition leaders pushed to negotiate a change of hours for the Guard members. It would not have been acceptable to let the guards go hungry, and we know they never would have stolen their food.

Accusations about bribery abound whenever competition is involved, and the Fair was no exception. Since thousands of juried competitions went on during the months of the Fair, there were not only plenty of sore losers and sour grapes, but also real cases of bribery. There were 100 protests over the selection of the famous

Yale Coffee, whose maker was accused of brewing up a scheme to pay off jurors at the coffee competition. The accusations proved to be accurate. In another case, Borden's Condensed Milk Co. took the LPE Co. to court and won a suit claiming that jury tampering had been going on when it received a silver medal instead of the gold.

Fraud

Sometimes the LPE Co. got taken. One extraordinary case was that of Mr. E. Judge, who was given the privilege of operating a 40,000-square-foot exhibit demonstrating how foods could be hermetically sealed. The display included machinery from the canning industry and a display of 2,000 firms engaged in the canning business. In an interview with the *Grocer World*, Judge said, "I believe that such education of the people will increase the consumption of the canned good by 50 percent among our best people, beside being likely to extend the market for American canned goods greatly to other countries." He said all the right things, including that he represented the national Association of Canned Good Manufacturers. The only problem was, there was no such association. There had been, but it had been defunct for seven years. Judge had apparently hoped that his association with such a reputable-sounding group would impress the Committee on Concessions to grant him an exhibit. He was right — at least until he was found out.

Accusations were made about the state food analysts who were involved in conducting an ongoing program of research for the Pure Food Movement. The editor of the *American Grocer* magazine accused both the state inspectors and state analysts of being incompetent and of using their positions to levy campaign funds for their own use. The editorial included the accusation that, instead of hiring expert chemists, they relegated the analyses to students.

Pennsylvania would have gotten "best in show" for "Fraud at the Fair." First of all, the exhibitors were kicked out of the Horticulture Building because they broke every official rule: fruits in the pomology section were rotting and not removed, greenery decorating the horticultural booth was wilted and brown, and fruit shipments were delayed or not picked up.

Although these Pennsylvania actions did not constitute fraud or graft, it did make Exposition inspectors suspicious, and they watched the Pennsylvania commissioners more carefully. In July, they were finally nabbed. The official rules directed that all exhibitors have authentic displays of their state's or country's products. Hoping not to be noticed, the Pennsylvania commissioner went to the St. Louis Seed Co. on 4th Street and bought $17.60 worth of seed. The seed was used to make a symbolic keystone (the state symbol) for Pennsylvania's exhibit in the Agriculture Building. It was marked, "Product of Pennsylvania." Whiskies purchased from Great Western Distillery in Peoria, Ill., were also displayed as "quality products from the Pennsylvania distilleries."

The boldest (or tackiest) action of all was displaying "Pennsylvania Cereal Products." Prominently displayed were boxes of Triscuits and Shredded Wheat (from the Natural Food Co. in Niagara Falls, N.Y.); Quaker Oats (from the American Cereal Co. of Chicago); Kellogg Postum and Grape Nuts (made in Battle Creek, Mich.); and Purina Flour (made at the Purina Mills in St. Louis). They were booted out of the Fair, and each man connected with the exhibit was considered a *persona non grata* in Pennsylvania. The Pennsylvania farmers back home demanded an investigation be done immediately because efforts to exhibit their products were repeatedly denied by the commissioners. We can imagine that the commissioners and the director of the exhibit weren't present at the Fair to handle these kinds of problems because we know that their incidental expenses included daily car rentals at $25 per day!

The LPE Co. prepared for the mismanagement of funds both for its own protection and for that of the concessionaires — especially the restaurants. Not all 25,000 wait staffers were brimming with late Victorian integrity. In order to get what was due in receipts, surprise "undercover" inspections were conducted by the Bureau of Inspections. Cash registers equipped with automatic adders were installed in the restaurants. Only the Exposition had the key to ensure that the tapes were not tampered with.

The bureau also implemented a now-familiar system in which each waiter's name was on the check — with an assigned identification number. At the end of the shift, the amount of the waiter's receipts and the amount given to the cashier had to match. Some of the more expensive restaurants hired independent companies to do the same services.

International Issues

For the most part, the world was at peace in 1904. Exhibitors who would be at war with each other within the next 10 years were following the same rules set by the Exposition. Some sent their children off to the Model Playground, where no color, shape of eye, or country of origin mattered much. It was, nevertheless, a time of extreme nationalism, one of the causes of the Great War just a few years away.

War was already going on between Russia and Japan, and it did not exist just between the two countries. It invaded every aspect of their dealings with others, and its effects were also felt at the Fair. Russia was taking the hardest hits back home, and, as a result, withdrew its participation in the Fair. The country kept the exhibits it had started, but did not fulfill its hopes of representing itself among the big names at the Fair — Germany, England, France, and even the fledgling United States.

Commissioner Alexandrovski of Russia had thought of a gift — one that was meant to last long after the lights were out in St. Louis. With Czar Nicholas' approval, Alexandrovski planned to establish the Russian pear tree in the United States. The bark of the Russian pear tree was unusually thick and afforded protection to the trees from the effects of very cold weather. The fruit also had a good flavor. He sent 1,000 seedlings over from the slopes and foothills of the Caucasus Mountains, had them planted on the fairgrounds, and planned to give away the saplings to fruit growers after the close of the World's Fair. The exhibit was installed in 1903 so that the trees would be hardy enough for the Fair, yet young enough to distribute after it was over. However, Russia lost sight of its fruitful project in St. Louis, and the distribution of trees never happened. No one in the U.S. picked up the sweet gesture, and we do not know what happened to the Russian pear trees. We only know that there are currently none in America.

> For the most part, the world was at peace in 1904. Exhibitors who would be at war with each other within the next 10 years were following the same rules set by the Exposition.

Primitive Food Fight

In July 1904, a reporter for the *Republic* gave an account of an undisputed food fight. It lasted very briefly. One of the cages for the Hagenbeck Wild Animal Show on the Pike housed a few monkeys and a fox terrier. While the residents of the cage were waiting to go on stage, a human onlooker threw a popcorn ball — most likely purchased from Popcorn Palace just a few concessions away — into the cage. The monkeys scrambled for possession of the ball, and the terrier jumped into the pile of chattering primates. One monkey lost a part of his tail in the process, and the dog got away with the popcorn ball!

Sarah Tyson Rorer

Not all of Mrs. Rorer's experiences at the Fair were as delicate as the delights she served to her guests. Although the minutes taken at an October 17, 1904 meeting aren't specific about the nature of Mrs. Rorer's complaint, she filed claim for $1,000 in damages to the LPE Co. A frequent complaint from restaurateurs was loss of income from some interruption of services, such as water, electricity, or gas, promised by the LPE Co. The committee ruled that, "her claim was not completely valid," but agreed to give her a $500 discount off her next payment due to the company.

This snapshot was taken of the animal cage where monkeys, dogs, and other animals awaited their part in the Hagenbeck Wild Animal Show. Courtesy Max Storm.

Mrs. Rorer had more problems than buildings and finances. She also encountered the human issues of her time, especially when she had to "break up a fight" between her employees. In the summer of 1904, the *Globe-Democrat* reported that, "The Greek coffee maker, Christan Papageorgacopoulon, threatened to resign his position if Mrs. Rorer did not satisfactorily resolve a situation in which a waitress, giving a hurry-up order, had called the Greek man by a derogatory term used for Italian immigrants. That was more than his sensitive nature could stand, and he demanded that the girl be disciplined for 'flippancy,' and be instructed as to the coffee maker's *nationality* (emphasis added)."

Because not everything was "sweet" at the Fair, Mrs. Rorer's desserts from her souvenir cookbook might have an especially nice appeal.

Fairies

"Put one quart of flour into a bowl, rub into it two ounces of butter and one teaspoonful of salt, now add sufficient cold water to make a rather stiff dough and knead and work continuously until the dough becomes soft, elastic, and is free from stickiness. Now roll it out on a board, and roll it as thin as a sheet of paper; cut with a round cutter, prick here and there with a fork, and bake about two or three minutes in a moderately hot oven."

Iced Chocolate

"Put six ounces of sweet chocolate into a boiler and stand it over boiling water to melt. Boil one-half cup of sugar and one-half pint of water until it forms a thick syrup. Scald one and one-half quarts of cream in a farina boiler, add it to the melted chocolate, then the syrup, mix thoroughly, and when cold, strain and freeze."

Plum Trifle

"Cut damsons into halves; remove the stones and press the pulp through a colander — they may be slightly heated first, if desired. Add to the half-pint of the pulp the well-beaten whites of four eggs. Fill a glass with sweetened cream, put the trifle over it by spoonfuls, heaping it up. Serve cold."

Lemon Frappé

"Add one pound of sugar to one quart of water; boil three minutes and skim. When cool, add the juice of four large lemons and the grated yellow rind of two, turn into a freezer, pack with salt and ice, allowing one quart of salt to ten pounds of ice. Turn the crank slowly and continuously until the mixture is half-frozen and looks like wet snow. Serve in lemonade glasses. … Nothing is more refreshing on a warm day, for lunch, than a nicely prepared frappé."

Leftovers

What do you do with a leftover pumpkin that weighs 180 pounds? How would you begin to get rid of a ton of maple sugar? While most of us worry about what to do with leftover turkey at Thanksgiving, the exhibitors and organizers at the Fair had far weightier problems. Not only did something have to be done with food each day, but also with all the food and materials that were left in the end. Millions of dollars worth of leftovers had to go somewhere, including booths, buildings, monuments — and even a Ferris Wheel!

Food leftovers were a daily occurrence. Tens of thousands of tons of food came through the Fair entrances. Plenty left in the bellies of tired visitors, but there were daily leftovers from the banquets, kitchens, exhibits, and restaurants. The food either had to be distributed or put into the waste dump. Some of the daily leftovers went to charity. For example, the Pillsbury-Washburn Co. managed to have a few biscuits, rolls, and doughnuts around at the end of the day, and those items went to local hospitals. Most of the daily leftovers went to personnel, however. The staff ate, took the leftovers home, or passed them on to friends from other exhibits.

> Not only did something have to be done with food each day, but also with all the food and materials that were left in the end.

Hauling the Garbage

Lots of leftovers ended up where most leftovers end up today — in the garbage. And Fair planners had given a lot of thought to that end of the food saga. Although it was not called the "Model Garbage Plant," the Garbage Crematory was considered so ideal that fairgoers could tour the plant.

Garbage pickup came with its own set of regulations. In the official *Rules for Disposal of Garbage on the Exposition Grounds*, the Division of Works made it clear that there would be no throwing waste of any kind in the lagoons, lakes, and waterways, on the grounds, or on the building floors. "All damp waste, scraps of vegetables, fruits, kitchen waste or slop must be placed in a galvanized cans with covers. Special means must be taken to prevent offense."

Those who had need for waste disposal were required to purchase double sets of cans for wet waste and double sets of sacks for dry waste, paying $5 for each can and $1 for each sack. The Exposition took the sacks and cans to the crematory for disposal and then cleaned and disinfected the cans before returning them to the owners. Pickup hours were between closing each night and 7:00 am, and every sack and can cost the vendor 20 cents each day. Any violation of the rules could cost the exhibitor or vendor his or her space.

Requests for Leftovers

Even before the Fair ended, the exhibitors received requests to purchase items seen in the booths of the palaces and national buildings. Some were genuine requests for purchase, and some inquirers were looking for a bargain.

Mr. Colvin Brown, who had spoken for Miss Juliana de Kol and had given the wedding party for a former resident of his home county, was in charge of the San Joachim County exhibit in the Palace of Agriculture. He received a request from Sara J. Turner of Mexico, Mo. "What would fifty pounds of San Joachim County soil, which I see in the *Republic* is the richest in the United States, cost? I want to put it in my flowerpots. Please let me know at once." Brown responded to her by saying that he was used to selling the soil by the acre and would find it hard to figure out what one pound would cost. He simply sent her 50 pounds compliments of the state of California. Henrietta Bowersten of Oregon asked for the same thing: "If you aren't doing anything with your soil, send it to me as I cannot raise anything in my back yard, and by spreading it [the soil] on, I think it would made the dirt rich enough for a good garden next summer." Brown had his secretary in California send her a box, too.

Even before the Fair ended, the exhibitors received requests to purchase items seen in the booths of the palaces and national buildings. Some were genuine requests for purchase, and some inquirers were looking for a bargain.

Final Generosity

At the end of the Fair, there were large quantities of display food that would have been too expensive to ship back to their places of origin. A generous helping of leftovers went to the benevolent societies in St. Louis, both sectarian and non-sectarian. The ton of maple sugar was distributed to charitable institutions at the behest of the Canadian Exhibit.

The operators of the Kings County, Calif., exhibit meant well when they sent a local St. Louis baker one of their supersized pumpkins weighing 180 pounds, figuring that the pumpkin could make 200 pumpkin pies. The Californians intended the pies to be sent to several of the local orphanages. It was perhaps a poor comparison to use with orphans when William Harris, representing the exhibit, said, "This pumpkin is a special variety and it will produce pies just like mother used to make."

One news story should bring a smile to the face of any native St. Louisan who remembers the annual Christmas drive of the *Post-Dispatch*. In December 1904, the *Post-Dispatch* ran a letter from the Argentine Commission at the Fair. The commission requested permission to disperse some of its inventory after the Fair by

Children from a local orphanage visited the Fair. Food exhibitors sent generous supplies of leftovers to many of these orphanages and other benevolent groups.

Courtesy Laura Brandt.

donating it to the Christmas Dinner for poor children that the *Post-Dispatch* sponsored. It offered its full display of biscuits, fruit preserves, caramels, butter, and other items. The record shows that the *Post-Dispatch* gladly accepted, and we can imagine the children did, too.

Leftovers for Sale

Not every food-related item ended up on the tables of the less fortunate in St. Louis. The Alameda (Calif.) County wine exhibitors sold 100 cases of their finest wines to the Missouri Athletic Club. The wines consisted of 23 varieties, including clarets, sauternes, ports, and Burgundies.

The restaurants themselves were sold, many for less than what a good bottle of wine would sell for today. One restaurant cost $6,000 to build and sold for $275. Another sold for $85. Some of the small lunchrooms in the exhibit halls were given away for the cost of removal.

For 25 cents, fence peepers could watch contractors from Chicago and St. Louis dismantle the palaces, the state buildings, and the restaurants.

To Keep or to Let Go

Some structures were planned from the beginning to be permanent, e.g., the Art Museum and the Bird Cage. But during the high-spirited moments of the Fair, there was talk of keeping the Model Playground that had proven so convenient for the working mothers of 1904. There was also a lot of talk about keeping the Pike. The administrator of Washington University across the street considered it for about five minutes and judged the whole idea quite unwise!

And so the Fair was scheduled to be dismantled. No doubt, it was hard to let go of a good thing, but winter was coming and the guests were heading home. Except for very few things, the Fair would disappear like Brigadoon — in clouds of dust created by the crumbling plaster and hemp that made it look so real. For 25 cents, fence peepers could watch contractors from Chicago and St. Louis dismantle the palaces, the state buildings, and the restaurants. Wood, nails, and anything else that could be turned into a profit went out the gates in nearly the same form as they had come in years before. Diane Rademacher's book, *Still Shining*, tracks some of the leftovers from the Fair to their new homes around the globe.

Treasuring the Leftovers

Thousand of souvenirs and millions of pieces of literature went home with visitors to the 1904 World's Fair: the Baker's Chocolate and Jell-O recipe booklets, the "Purina bags," the Incubator Restaurant menu, stereopticon views of the prune bear, and Fairy Floss wrappers. Like leftover food in modern refrigerators, the World's Fair visitor intended to reuse them in some creative way — scrapbooking or giving them to the kids as a legacy. But, like so many leftovers, many of these items eventually were found to be clutter and in the way of household efficiency, and many were tossed into the garbage.

Lucky for some, there were the "benevolent societies" for these kinds of leftovers from the World's Fair — the St. Louis City Library and the Missouri Historical Society. In these places, the people who continue to protect the 100-year-old leftovers are hard at work: Jean Gosebrink and Tom Pearson from the St. Louis Central Library's Special Collections provide information and make countless trips to the archives and carry fragile scrapbooks back to researchers hungry for the truth about food at the 1904 World's Fair. The director of library and archives at the Missouri Historical Society, Duane Sneddeker, makes it possible to view both familar and rare photos of the Fair.

Some of the leftovers remain, however, safely in the hands of individuals. These creative and imaginative people can hold these mementos and imagine what they meant to people and a city experiencing a gentler side of human history in the 20th century. St. Louis World's Fair Society collectors, Max Storm, Pat Villmer, Louise Drescher, Mike Truax, and Yvonne Suess, and Pan-American Exposition collector, Fred Lavin, did for this book what the exhibitors were commissioned to do with their booths: "Give it life; give it motion." The best descriptions and information about Fairy Floss could never spark the imagination or take anyone back in time like the authentic packaging of the Fairy Floss. With a rare picture of the ice cream cone or a signed copy of Mrs. Rorer's *World's Fair Souvenir Cook Book*, these generous collectors prove that "leftovers" can be treasures.

after the Fair
was over

Sarah Tyson Rorer

Children and the young at heart have always found creative uses for things cast off by the less imaginative. During the winter of 1904-1905, when the Fair was being demolished, both children and adults used restaurant chairs to sled down Art Hill (located in front of the Art Museum in Forest Park). These were the first sleigh riders on the hill, and they were probably unaware that their playful movements would

Sledders used Mrs. Rorer's restaurant as a starting point to sled down Art Hill. The chairs used for sleds were most likely from Mrs. Rorer's East Pavilion Cafe.

Jessie Tarbox Beals, courtesy Missouri Historical Society, St. Louis.

start a tradition that has been sustained for 100 years. After every big snow, the city of St. Louis's television stations drag their equipment over to Art Hill to record the time-honored custom of sledding. Little do the sledders know that they begin their ride on the very spot where a restaurant stood 100 years ago — Sarah Tyson Rorer's East Pavilion Cafe.

Mrs. Rorer was probably not the one who thought of the "chair-sled," but she would have been very pleased with the economical and clever use of her chairs. Mrs. Rorer believed in economy. She lectured on it frequently and even included a specific chapter on leftovers in *Mrs. Rorer's My Best 250 Recipes* (1907).

Although her *World's Fair Souvenir Cook Book* did not include a specific chapter on leftovers, she did have recipes that made good use of leftovers, and they are included here. The bread pudding recipe is from *Mrs. Rorer's My Best 250 Recipes*.

Author's collecction.

MY BEST TWENTY LEFT-OVERS

True economy consists of buying small quantities of the best materials and using them carefully. When one wants a fine piece of roasted beef the roast itself must be of fair size; small roasts are extravagant and not palatable. Large roasts lose less in cooking than small ones, but the left-overs must be utilized or the dish is most expensive. As a rule left-overs are extravagances; they show thoughtless buying; but to know how to utilize them is the stronghold of every housewife. Many left-over vegetables are better on second cooking, especially the starchy ones. Not so, however, with meats.

Dishes made from eggs and milk should not be kept for a second day, especially during the warm months. Fish, even if perfectly fresh when cooked, is by far more dangerous than stale meat. Beef and mutton keep longer than either fish or white meats.

A few of the succulent vegetables, such as beans, peas, corn and stewed tomatoes, are better the second day than on the first; enough may be cooked one day to serve for the second, providing they are quickly chilled after cooking. Stock and

Boudins

"Chop cold cooked chicken fine, measure, and to every pint add a table-spoonful of butter, two tablespoonfuls of dried bread-crumbs, half a cup of stock or boiling water, two eggs, slightly beaten, salt and pepper to taste. Put all these ingredients into a saucepan and stir over the fire for a moment until thoroughly mixed. Fill custard cups two-thirds full with this mixture, stand them in a baking-pan half-filled with boiling water, and bake in a moderate oven twenty minutes. When done turn them out carefully on a heated dish and pour around them cream of Béchamel Sauce. Remains of cold roast or boiled poultry can be used this way."

Bread Pudding

"Beat two eggs without separating, add four tablespoonfuls of sugar, and beat again; add one pint of milk, half a tea-spoonful of salt, a grating of nutmeg; pour into a baking-dish, cover the top with buttered bread, buttered side up, and bake in a moderate oven until the custard is set (about twenty minutes). Serve cold."

Potato Puff

"Put a pint of cold mashed pota-toes in a saucepan; add half a cupful of milk; stir, and beat until the potatoes are hot and smooth. Take from the fire; fold in the well-beaten whites of two eggs, heap in a baking-dish, and brown quickly in a hot oven. Serve with roasted or broiled beef."

Fond "Adieu"

The quartet in the gallery of the Tyrolean Alps sang, "For Here's[sic] a Jolly Good Fellow" to the man seated at the table in the center of the main dining hall. He had been there many times before to honor so many others, but this day and night was his. Dec. 1, 1904, the last day of the Fair, was Francis Day, and David R. Francis was the sole honoree noted in the *Daily Official Program.*

In some ways, Dec. 1, 1904 was business as usual — a series of banquets, receptions, and dinners — but the toasts, the ovations, the thanks, the applause, and the speeches recognized Francis's Herculean efforts to arrange a national and international event of this magnitude.

During the day, the foreign commissioners had walked to his office two abreast to thank him for a job well done and for the pleasant relationships he had maintained with them throughout the Fair. He returned the compliment and assured them that their nations would be proud of their representation at the Fair. The Board of Lady Managers held a fine reception in its decorated salons for President Francis and the Board of Directors. They had managed to work well together and get beyond their differences.

The afternoon event was a little more out of the ordinary, and was probably an amazing experience for all involved. Francis and the Board of Directors — Frederick Skiff, Frederic Taylor, Isaac Taylor, and the others — rode on the Yellowstone Park Coach through all the streets of the fairgrounds one last time. They were greeted by an unbroken stream of claps and cheers!

Although he'd gone in and out of the Tyrolean Alps Restaurant for dinner hundreds of times, the last four hours of the Fair made that simple act anything but simple.

The first page from the Daily Official Program *on December 1, 1904, Francis Day. The day was filled with celebratory events honoring Fair President Francis.*

Courtesy Max Storm.

Mounted police had to "charge" the crowd surrounding the Alps so that Francis and his party could get to the dining hall for the closing banquet. Once safely there, his short speech expressed what he believed so many thought and felt: If the world could only have the Fair for just one more year!

Later on that night, when he reached the plaza of St. Louis and stood under the Louisiana Purchase Monument, 100,000 people surrounded him to say fond "adieu" to the Fair and to Francis. Millions of lights were shining, as they had been every night, when Francis spoke. "I am about to perform a heartrending duty." He said Congress had given him no choice but to close the Fair. To the crowds who had heard him speak on hundreds of occasions, Francis's quivering voice was not familiar and may have left them at a loss. But at one of Francis's later remarks the crowd "went crazy" and clapped for two minutes: He had turned and put his hand on the arm of his wife who stood next to him. "Here stands the partner of my life. Mrs. Francis and I have been blessed with six sons. If I were called on to lose one of them tomorrow, the only consolation I could find would be the record he left behind him. So, when we are called upon to lose the great Exposition, the only consolation left to us is the record it leaves behind it."

With that, Francis approached the switch that would turn out the electric lights "Farewell," he said. "A long farewell to all thy splendor." The familiar outline of lights dimmed, and the entire fairgrounds were darkened. Lighting them again were fireworks that spelled, "Farewell and Good Night."

It was after midnight, and time to go home.

The view of Festival Hall, the Colonnade, and the east and west restaurant pavilions at night. The lights went out for good just before midnight on December 1, 1904.
Courtesy Max Storm.

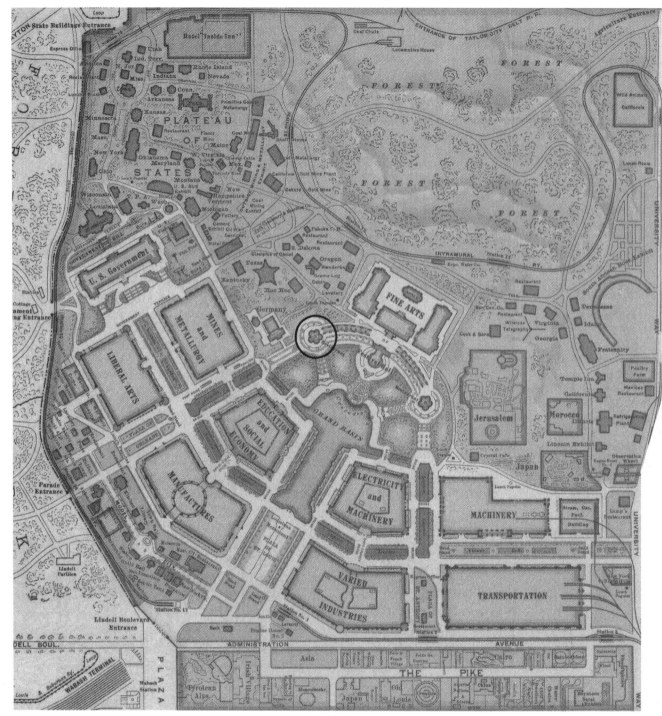

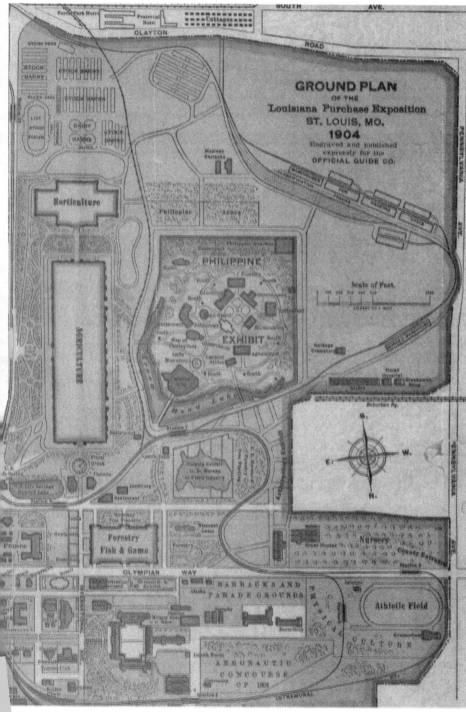

Fairgoers purchased official guidebooks with foldout maps like this one. Visitors relied on maps like these to navigate through miles of Fair attractions, locate eateries, and find railway transportation home.

Mrs. Rorer's East Pavilion Restaurant (circled) is located to the left of Festival Hall in the center part of the map on page 172.

Author's collection

Books

Bennitt, Mark, ed. *History of the Louisiana Purchase Exposition.* St. Louis: Universal Exposition Publishing Co., 1905.

Buel, J.W., ed. *Louisiana and the Fair: An Exposition of the World, Its People and Their Achievements.* 10 vols. St. Louis: World's Progress Publishing Co., 1904-1905.

Clevenger, Martha. *"Indescribably Grand":* Diaries and Letters From the 1904 World's Fair. St. Louis: Missouri Historical Society Press, 1996.

Everett, Marshall. *The Book of the Fair.* St. Louis: P.W. Ziegler Co., 1904.

Fox, Timothy J. and Sneddeker, Duane R. *From the Palaces to the Pike: Visions of the 1904 World's Fair.* St. Louis: Missouri Historical Society Press, 1997.

Francis, David R. *The Universal Exposition of 1904.* 2 vols. St. Louis: Louisiana Purchase Co., 1913.

Lowenstein, M.J., ed. *Official Guide to the Louisiana Purchase Exposition.* St. Louis: The Official Guide Co., 1904.

Official Catalogue of Exhibits. St. Louis: Official Catalogue Co., Louisiana Purchase Exposition, 1904.

Official Louisiana Purchase Exposition, Official Photographers. St. Louis: The Official Photographic Co., 1904.

Stevens, Walter. *The World's Fair: Official Photographic Work of the Universal Exposition St. Louis.* St. Louis: N.D. Thompson Publishing Co., 1903.

Weigley, Emma. *Sarah Tyson Rorer: The Nation's Instructress in Dietetics and Cookery.* Philadelphia: The American Philosophical Society, 1977.

World's Fair Authentic Guide. St. Louis: The Official Guide Co., 1904.

Newspapers

St. Louis Post-Dispatch

December 1903-December 1904.

"The Fare at the Fair," Sept. 9, 1968.

"Melting Claims on the First Ice Cream Cone," June 4, 1978.

St. Louis Republic

April 1904-December 1904.

St. Louis Globe-Democrat

April 1904-December 1904.

Periodicals

Walker, John Brisben, ed. *The Cosmopolitan* (April-September, 1904).

Page, Walter, ed. *The World's Work* (August 1904).

Archives and Special Collections

Missouri Historical Society Library and Archives

• Louisiana Purchase Exposition Collection (Records of the Louisiana Purchase Exposition Co., Box 13, Folders 1–7), 1901–1904.

• Louisiana Purchase Exposition Scrapbooks, vols. 7, 8, 14–16, 21, 25, 35, 36, 50, 51, 60-63, 91, 92, 114, 162–164, 194, 198; 1901–1904.

• Final Report of the Louisiana Purchase Exposition Commission, 1906.

• Selph, Colin, ed. *World's Fair Bulletin* (February-December 1904).

St. Louis Public Library Special Collections

• Louisiana Purchase Exposition Scrapbooks; Frederic W. Taylor, Director of Agriculture and Horticulture, vols. 1,4–7,13,14,16. 1903–1904.

Internet

www.lyndonirwin.com/1904agri.htm

www.boondocksnet.com

www.users.vnet.net/schulman/Columbian/Columbian.html

www.Gti.net

www.buffalo.edu/libraries/exhibits/panam/food/marvels.html

www.whatscookingamerica.com

www.idfa.org

www.hot-dog.org

www.inventors.about.com